Teaching the 3 Cs

Creativity, Curiosity, and Courtesy

Activities That Build a Foundation for Success

Patricia A.
Dischler

CORWIN
A SAGE Company

For information:

Corwin
A SAGE Company
2455 Teller Road
Thousand Oaks, California 91320
(800) 233-9936
Fax: (800) 417-2466
www.corwinpress.com

SAGE India Pvt. Ltd.
B 1/I 1 Mohan Cooperative
    Industrial Area
Mathura Road, New Delhi 110 044
India

SAGE Ltd.
1 Oliver's Yard
55 City Road
London EC1Y 1SP
United Kingdom

SAGE Asia-Pacific Pte. Ltd.
33 Pekin Street #02-01
Far East Square
Singapore 048763

Printed in the United States of America.

Library of Congress Cataloging-in-Publication Data

Dischler, Patricia A.
Teaching the 3 Cs : creativity, curiosity, and courtesy : activities that build a foundation for success / Patricia A. Dischler.
      p. cm.
Includes bibliographical references and index.
ISBN 978-1-4129-7422-6 (pbk.)
    1. Early childhood education—Activity programs. 2. Creative activities and seat work. 3. Social interaction—Study and teaching (Early childhood) I. Title.

LB1139.35.A37D57 2010
372.21—dc22   2009023348

This book is printed on acid-free paper.

09   10   11   12   13   10   9   8   7   6   5   4   3   2   1

Acquisitions Editor:	Jessica Allan
Editorial Assistant:	Joanna Coelho
Production Editor:	Eric Garner
Copy Editor:	John Vias
Typesetter:	C&M Digitals (P) Ltd.
Proofreader:	Joyce Li
Indexer:	Sheila Bodell
Cover Designer:	Rose Storey
Graphic Designer:	Karine Hovsepian

Contents

Acknowledgments

I would first like to thank all the parents who entrusted me with their children during the 17 years I operated Patty Cake Preschool. The title of this book was the slogan for my school, and the fact that so many of you saw the value in teaching these concepts to your children is why I decided to share these ideas in book form.

I'd like to thank my husband, Steve, for all his love and support during this project. For once again understanding as I spent our weekends pouring through research, and our nights in my office. For listening attentively as I read him each chapter and trying to give the best feedback he could, considering his background is in construction and not early childhood! For understanding why the gourmet dinners he married me for were replaced briefly with hotdogs and Kraft Macaroni and Cheese. For buying me a record player for Christmas so I could play my soundtracks of *Mary Poppins* and *The Music Man* to get my creative juices flowing again. I love you, and your confidence in my abilities is what pushes me to complete all my goals.

I would like to thank those who helped me find the resources necessary to complete this book—the staffs of the Prairie du Sac Public Library and the Wisconsin Child Care Information Center. Thank you all so much for not fainting when I handed you a two-page list of books I wanted!

Thank you to all the child care professionals, teachers, and family child care providers who have shared their ideas with me over the years; I learned so very much from all of you. Many of the activities in this book were inspired by your presentations at conferences and other trainings or handed down from you to many others until the idea came up at a meeting I attended. We are all in this together, and the wealth of ideas shared among professionals is what inspires us all to give it our best.

And finally, thank you to Jessica Allan at Corwin, who was curious about my manuscript and kind enough to discuss my goals before making a final decision. I am so very grateful for this opportunity to share this information and to partner with a wonderful publishing company like Corwin.

Additionally, Corwin would like to acknowledge the following peer reviewers for their editorial insight and guidance:

Michelle Barnea
Executive Director
Early Learning Innovations LLC
Millburn, New Jersey

Angie Bonthuis
Kindergarten Teacher, NBCT
Gilbert Community School District
Gilbert, Iowa
www.ilovekindergarten.com

Carrie Clark
First Grade Teacher
Gilbert Community Schools
Ames, Iowa

Darlene Wontrop
Literacy Leader
International Reading Association
Harford County Public Schools
Forest Hill, Maryland

About the Author

**Patricia A. Dischler** is an author, speaker, and educator sharing her 20 years of experience in the field of early childhood education and 17 years as owner of Patty Cake Preschool, a nationally accredited family child care business. The author of several books, including *From Babysitter to Business Owner*, *Because I Loved You*, and *The Patty Cake Kids and the Lost Imagination Cap*, she speaks nationally at early childhood and adoption conferences and is a columnist for *National Perspective*, the newsletter of the National Association for Family Child Care (NAFCC), and *Adoption Today* magazine. Patricia is an executive board member of the NAFCC, Wisconsin Family Child Care Association, and the Wisconsin Early Learning Coalition and was the recipient of the 2007 Wisconsin Governor's Award for excellence in the field of child care. To learn more, visit her Web site at www.patriciadischler.com.

To Mom

Thank you for your endless creativity, your infectious curiosity, and all of the little courtesies you bestowed on our family over the years. You inspire me.

Introduction

In the world of early childhood, there has been an increase in the pressure to teach the traditional three *Rs*: Reading, 'Riting, and 'Rithmetic. What was once the curriculum for first grade has become the standard for kindergarten classrooms, and what was once a kindergarten lesson is expected at the preschool level. Parents feel they should expect more, and research shows kids are capable of more, so standards get tighter, and the pressure is on for early childhood teachers and parents to deliver. The unfortunate result of this has been early childhood programs and parents that focus on getting the academic results but leave behind the basics for all learning. It is no surprise, then, that many programs are struggling and that children in higher grades are being found to have additional problems with social interactions and little or no problem-solving techniques. The missing link? Teaching the three *Cs*. Instilling in children a love for learning, a process for making decisions, and the ability to solve problems while working with others begins by encouraging their creativity, curiosity, and courtesy.

The days for simple play and exploration in childhood seem to be gone. But in order for the new programs of advanced learning and the parents of these children to be effective in any way, children must be allowed the opportunity to build a basis for all learning, to get excited about what the possibilities are and what their part in it will be.

Teaching creativity to children is not only fun for the children, teachers, and parents, it opens doors to other learning. By letting children explore new possibilities with materials, activities, and discussions, they can become masters of their own learning. Children have a natural curiosity, but all too often it is quieted by a predisposed lesson plan or a busy personal schedule. Teachers and parents who follow a child's natural curiosity and provide them the avenues to obtain the information they crave will find that more learning takes place in those moments than in a week's worth of planned activities. As children interact with each other and adults, modeling and requiring a standard of courtesy creates a sense of respect among all. Children who show respect and feel it from others will have strong self-esteem and build successful relationships with peers and adults.

Part 1 of this book will address creativity. It's not so much a matter of "teaching" creativity as it is allowing for creative moments to happen and expanding on them when they do. We'll discuss what makes a creative person and what attributes we can enhance to bring out the creativeness in all children. Then you'll be provided with activities that help to foster creativity in children. Next, there will be activities that can integrate creativity into the standards set by many states for early childhood assessment. These will help ensure a teacher's ability to meet these standards but also create a basis for this learning by integrating creativity into the activities.

Part 2 focuses on curiosity. We'll discuss the importance of curiosity and how it supports further learning. We'll explore the connection between curiosity and creativity, the natural abilities of children to be curious, and the dangers in containing this curiosity. You'll be provided with activities that foster creativity and also those that integrate it into the developmental standards.

Finally, we'll explore courtesy. We'll discuss how we as teachers and parents are key in supporting this attribute through our modeling. Manners in general have undergone many changes in our society over the years, so we'll take a look at the character aspects that still stand strong. I'll share activities that promote courtesy in children as well as those that are integrated into further learning.

Activities will be listed under the standards they will meet. The standards categories chosen for the activities are based on the standards list from the National Institute for Early Education Research (NIEER). A complete list of the standard areas and underlying categories can be found by searching for "state standards" at http://nieer.org. Those using the Creative Curriculum will also find that their "50 Goals and Objectives" fall within these identified standards as well. The standards categories you will find in this book are

- Language and literacy
- Math
- Science
- Social and emotional, which includes social studies
- Cognitive development, including memory, the senses, and problem solving
- Health and physical development
- The arts, including visual art, music, and drama

In addition to the standard areas identified by NIEER, I have included "the arts," an identified content area of the Creative Curriculum. Unfortunately, this content area has not been identified by NIEER, most likely because it is not found in the state standards used to compile their lists. This further demonstrates the importance of working to add this aspect of creative content to our curriculums, so it will be included in the standards listed for each *C*.

Currently, every U.S. state and the District of Columbia have adopted some form of early learning standards. These standards drive a teacher's curriculum but do not define it. In *The Curriculum Bridge: From Standards to Actual Classroom Practice*, author Pearl G. Solomon (2003) reports that teachers have control over curriculum. They are influenced by state standards and effects of power and school organization, but ultimately they use these as a base from which to build their own curriculums. "With consistency in the content and performance standards as the objective, teachers can be creative, responsive, and timely with the activities they use to achieve the standards" (p. 90). She points out that "there is often more than one way to solve a problem and more than one way to reach a standard" (p. 89).

The purpose of this book is to help parents, teachers, and child care providers—anyone who works with young children—create a basis for further learning. By learning how to work with children on enhancing their natural abilities to be creative, curious, and courteous, as well as using these abilities to accomplish other developmental goals, we not only give our children a foundation but help them to begin the process of constructing their future.

Teaching Creativity 1

Sparking creativity in children opens the door to learning in every developmental area. When children think creatively, they look beyond what is in front of them to see what could be. They explore from many different angles and engage all their senses. This creative exploration can lead to successful problem solving, a broader understanding of topics taught, and a sense of appreciation for the world they live in.

To "teach" creativity is to embed a child's day with options—to provide the physical environment to support creative action as well as the psychological environment to support the quest. For teachers and parents, this means not only providing appropriate materials but also creating an atmosphere that encourages the exploration of new ideas.

Rather than separate creativity from other concepts being taught to the child, creativity is best fostered when it becomes an underlying standard in all play and learning.

For children to excel in a variety of academic areas, they need an established basis for exploring new information, understanding it thoroughly, and using what they know to problem solve. This basis is creativity.

Thinking creatively allows children to open their minds to further learning. Without this basis of thinking creatively, children are prone to merely *acquire* information—rather than have the skill to *do* something with this information. When children are supported in their creativity, they are able to actively engage in the learning process. For example, it is more than learning there *are* numbers, but about learning what those numbers are capable of *doing*—how they interact, what they represent, and how they are used to organize or represent objects and information.

Creativity puts further learning and exploration in motion, involving much more than art projects. In *More Help! For Teachers of Young Children*, author Gwen Snyder (2006) encourages teachers to look beyond the art project as their avenue for supporting creativity in children. She states, "The outstanding musician, writer, teacher, engineer, architect, scientist, athlete, inventor, business leader, and chef all have at least one thing in common. They are willing to look at the world with fresh eyes, to step beyond the way things have always been done and dare to imagine how they can be done differently. This is the very core of creativity" (p. 155).

As teachers and parents, we need to remember this advice. Creativity is not simply art expression. It is the expression of all ideas, emotions, and desires and can manifest itself through many diverse mediums from writing to engineering and beyond.

To support children in stretching their creative muscles, parents and teachers can begin by simply trusting that they can and will find their way on their own. Too often, adults feel the need to lead children—they want to protect them from disappointment, harm, and conflict, so they try their best to show them the "right" way. But this robs children of the opportunity to learn from their experiences, to follow their hearts, and to trust their own instincts.

Parents and teachers who trust their children to embrace the process and find their own answers not only open the children's minds creatively but also support their sense of self-esteem and empowerment. As adults show trust in children, children will increase their trust in their own instincts. Following creative instinct, and feeling supported and trusted during this process, will allow children's trust in their own ideas to grow and increase their level of creative thought.

In *The Nurturing Parent: How to Raise Creative, Loving, Responsible Children,* authors John Dacey and Alex Packer (2006) studied highly creative children and identified a particular parenting style that supported this growth of creativity. They called it the "nurturing parent." While they identified many aspects that contributed to the parent's ability to support their child's creativity, they state "perhaps more than anything, nurturing parents *trust*" (p. 17).

These nurturing parents differed from other parents "in that they tend to be more consistent in dealing with their children, and more willing to let them learn through experience. They believe that children get better at the things they practice . . . that they must make their own decisions if they are to learn good judgment" (Dacey & Packer, 1992, p. 17). These parents recognized that when adults make decisions for children, it teaches the children not to trust their own instincts, but when adults show trust in children, the children learn to trust their own decisions.

This does not mean that we back away altogether and let children wander aimlessly looking for answers. Rather, we become part of the background of their experience, providing information, props, and encouragement along the way to support their quests. A child trying to build a fort, for example, may see a branch he or she feels would work just right, but the child needs an adult to get it down. Or the child may wonder aloud how big a blanket it will take to cover the top, and the parent could provide a tape measure. As the work progresses, the adult can provide support through verbal encouragement such as, "The stick you used across the top fits just right!"

A word of caution here: Providing encouragement is very different from praise. Research shows that excessive praise for children's actions leads them to seek more praise and approval—they begin to discount their own feelings and give weight only to the feelings of others. Dacey and Packer (1992) contend that "nothing destroys creativity faster than praise" (p. 39).

The encouragement children need is in trusting their feelings of accomplishment. By expressing praise for children's *efforts* and allowing them to voice their opinions on the *result* of that effort, you are empowering children to analyze their efforts and trust in their own sense of pride. Once children have expressed their own reactions, praise, and criticisms, then it is appropriate for the adults to express their own. At this point it simply *adds to* the children's perspective of the result. Through this type of encouragement, parents and teachers can show children the rewards that result from their sense of purpose—the excitement of pride and accomplishment—rather than focusing on praise, money, stickers, or other outside rewards. Teach children to see their self-pride as its own reward, and one worth striving for.

Creative thinking often leads to actions that exercise independence. As children begin to trust their creative thought processes, they will feel more empowered to step away from the crowd. Actions of independence should be valued and encouraged. Independence allows creative thought to blossom uninhibited and leads children to answers that are new and exciting— not just for them but for those around them!

The ability to find new and exciting answers is often described as "thinking outside the box." It is used to describe creative people or to encourage adults to think creatively. But what exactly does it take to think outside the box? Several factors affect creative thinking:

- Functional freedom
- Stimulus freedom
- Delayed gratification
- Balanced-brain thinking

Parents and teachers can support creative thinking by providing activities that support these four factors. Together, they give children the tools they need to explore their world with a creative eye and come to their own conclusions regarding their place in the world and their ability to change it.

FUNCTIONAL FREEDOM

When we teach functional freedom, we are showing children the world of possibilities—a box may be something more than just a box. We are letting their imaginations dictate the use of an object rather than letting the object dictate its use.

How children express their creativity through imagination can be different for each child and for each situation. As parents or teachers, knowing your children's personalities—what's important to them, what excites them—can help you lend support to how they express creativity. For example, knowing your child's love of airplanes, you can provide small toy airplanes for him or her to use when working on math as a means for expressing math problems and solutions. The planes become representations of numbers. Another child may feel creative freedom in making up a song about numbers, and another in writing a book about them.

Looking over your environment and ensuring it is conducive to supporting the creativity of the children in it will help in offering moments of functional freedom thoughts to them. Provide props that excite and inspire the children—things they know and love as well as items that are new and spark their curiosity. In *The A to Z Guide to Raising Happy, Confident Kids*, author Jenn Berman (2007) tells us that "of all our different personality characteristics, creativity is most influenced by the child's environment" (p. 171).

A wonderful educator in Wisconsin, Inez Learn, told a group of teachers at her creativity workshop[1] that when purchasing toys for their day care, to ask themselves if the play is in the toy or in the child. If the toy can do its thing all by itself, then what's the kid for? To sit and watch? But if it takes a child to manipulate the toy, to give it a name, to declare it is going somewhere or feeling something, then it's really doing something. Too often we try to give children what looks like fun when all they really want is the box! They naturally think in functionally free ways. What kids need isn't for you to tell them what or how to play but to simply give them the opportunity to do it. Their own imaginations will power the play and lead them to places you probably would never dream of. Unless, that is, you've worked to maintain a bit of your own creativity. Then you might have a fighting chance to join in.

Pose the same question when looking over your child's environment, whether it is a bedroom or playroom at home, or your classroom or day care room. Is the play in the environment or the child? Does it take *action* from the child to make something happen? Does it take decisions and imagination, or is the play all laid out for them? Think of children's play-time like a theatrical play—you don't want to be the director and give them their lines. You want to be a prop man. Make them the play-wrights. Just be sure they have what they need to keep the play moving into the next act!

In thinking of children's environments, we must also include the out-door spaces they inhabit. Unfortunately, for many children, outdoor space may be limited to playgrounds and manicured parks. In *Last Child in the Woods,* author Richard Louv (2005) declares that the new generation of children will face what he calls "nature-deficit disorder." He notes this is not a medical diagnosis, but a way to think about the problem. His theory, based on interviews with over 3,000 children and parents, is that this generation of children has no personal relationship with nature and that this is creating a deficit in a child's ability to learn certain concepts.

One of these concepts is creativity. Louv (2005) states, "Nature inspires creativity in a child by demanding visualization and the full use of the senses" (p. 7). Many researchers are confirming this theory. Sebastiano Santostefano (2005), director of the Massachusetts Psychology Institute, said, "If you [use] traditional puppets and games, there are lim-its. A policeman puppet is usually a policeman; a kid rarely makes it some-thing else. But with landscape, it's much more engaging, and you're giving the child ways of expressing what's within" (pp. 51 52). Nature provides so much to support a child's sense of functional freedom. It offers items that provide a variety of sensory experiences, all subject to a child's interpretation and imagination. Sensory experiences are vital to creativity. Nature encourages the use of all senses, as opposed to television and most toys, which engage only sight and sound. Nature fills the need for the healthy development of children's senses and therefore supports the development of creativity.

Our country has evolved into a place where the child has been dis-connected from nature. Whereas the learning used to be within the child—creating forts, building dams in creeks, and other play in nature—the learning is now orchestrated by adults. Parents build tree houses that follow covenant rules based on a plan from their home improvement store. Adults build play structures at parks and public pools with water play components they have designed. We've forgotten that what the children gained from these play situations was not the end result—it was the process. With the process taken away, it is no surprise that a drive through neighborhoods will show you many play structures and parks where chil-dren are nowhere to be seen.

Years ago, as a new teacher at a child care center, I was initially impressed with the massive play structure in the playground. However, in a short time, I saw that it had one major flaw—there were no moving parts. It was simply a big thing. It could not be manipulated by the children and therefore they found no fun in it. I noticed how the children spent more time around it, playing in the dirt at the end of the slide, picking the flowers that grew near it, and scooping the woodchips around it than they did actually on the structure. Taking my cue from them, I packed up my group and walked across the street to an empty lot that had a beautiful meadow. We crawled on our bellies in the grass like snakes, picked flowers and counted their petals, watched caterpillars crawl on leaves, caught butterflies, and used sticks to build a fort. After doing this every day for several days, I was brought into my director's office and almost fired.

I was told that it was inappropriate to take the children outside of our center, to "wander around a dirty empty lot," and to not follow our strict guidelines for time outside. It was obvious to me this director did not see the value of nature. As a farm girl from Iowa, I knew it very well. I soon decided to open a family day care business of my own where, I'm proud to say, we spent every day exploring meadows and other wonderful aspects of nature to our hearts' content.

That children need to manipulate their environment is more than my personal observation. Ben Nicholson, Britain's most prominent twentieth-century artist, brought this need to the attention of all educators when he posed his "loose-parts theory." He states, "In any environment, both the degree of inventiveness and creativity, and the possibility of discovery, are directly proportional to the number and kind of variables in it" (cited in Louv, 2005, p. 86). In other words, when kids get to manipulate objects, it sparks their creativity and imagination.

We still have many constraints in letting our children build a relationship with nature. But we can use this information to help us make better choices for supporting this relationship—taking our children to parks and other places where they are allowed to wander freely, to explore, to pick flowers, and to manipulate objects; providing them space in our own yards and playgrounds where it is okay to dig and build; building play structures that provide them manipulative experiences; and adding props that take this even further. More than just a support for creative minds, Louv (2005) shares with us his research findings that "environment-based education produces student gains in social studies, science, language arts, and math; improves standardized test scores and grade point averages; and develops skills in problem-solving, critical thinking and decision making" (p. 204).

Providing "loose parts" for our children and allowing them to use their imaginations to combine these parts or see them as new objects often results in messiness. However, this messiness should be celebrated as a reflection of learning! In *Natural Playscapes: Creating Outdoor Play Environments for the Soul*, author Rusty Keeler (2008) discusses the importance of messiness in regard to creativity and how these activities work to create a basis for further learning. "Childhood is supposed to be messy and natural playscapes (outdoor play areas) offer a kind of messiness that inspires learning and creativity. The skills they learn on the playscape, such as having the confidence to try things they've never done before, will later translate to the school setting" (p. 282).

Functional freedom allows children to stretch their creative muscles, to consider what was not considered before. Dacey and Packer (1992) point out that "functionally free kids are easy to recognize. They are the ones who pipe up with the simple solution that went over everyone's head" (p. 54).

A great example of this is the time I had a problem with children jumping over the couch in my classroom. I had the couch set with the side against a wall, creating a barrier between two areas in the room. However, the children seemed compelled to jump over the back of the couch when going from the one area to another. Rules and consequences seemed to have no effect on curbing this behavior. So one morning at group time, I posed this question: "What will it take for you to stop jumping over the couch?"

Four-year-old Hannah gave me a "duh" roll of the eyes and shrugged as she answered, "If there was something on the other side, I wouldn't be able to jump over it."

That had definitely gone right over my head! I was so busy thinking of the functional use of the couch—to be sat on—I didn't consider its use as a jumping item, which made it impossible for me to think of a way for it *not* to work as a jumping item. Hannah saw it as something to jump over, which led to thinking of reasons why it wouldn't work as something to jump over, which led to her solution. By being functionally free, she was able to follow a thought process I wasn't able to and find the solution. We moved a bookcase to the back side of the couch, placed a plant and the fishbowl on top, and that was the end of the jumping.

Supporting this type of thought process means being open to all the possibilities for our props, environ-

Ethan and I were working on opposites and I asked him what was the opposite of *up*. He replied, "Going to bed!"

ments, and natural play areas for children. By doing so, we are supporting their imagination and sense of functional freedom. Their creativity blossoms and they discover more about themselves, their world, and each other.

STIMULUS FREEDOM

Stimulus freedom is another important factor in supporting children's imagination and creativity. It means not assuming there are rules to follow, or that if there are, knowing they can be bent. It means understanding the *reasoning* behind the rules so that children can understand the possibilities of changing rules to meet the needs of new situations and priorities. It also means not being afraid of making a mistake, of breaking a rule, or trying to do something in a way that is different from the process previously used.

Stimulus freedom allows children to place a high value on the *process* rather than the *results.* A current television commercial is a great illustration of this. An inventor of a vacuum cleaner explains how it took 2,000 prototypes before they got it right. He talks about how they would get excited each time one didn't work because it meant they had discovered something new; they had identified what not to do and this led them closer to what to do. Wouldn't it be great if we all got so excited about doing things that didn't work out? Recognizing that each step in a process is a potential for learning is exciting! Show your child that you value this more than the results, for if it were not for the process there would be no result.

Dr. Jenn Berman (2007) tells us that "young children naturally have the curiosity and confidence to try new things until they become self-conscious and afraid to make mistakes" (p. 171). When adults portray mistakes as a negative part of the process, children begin to question themselves, and rather than embracing a mistake as an opportunity to learn, they feel ashamed by them and hide them, learning nothing in the process.

Parents and teachers who celebrate these mistakes as parts of the process can help empower children to trust their instincts and move forward with confidence, unafraid of making a new mistake because they will see it as a step in the process rather than a roadblock. Robert Kennedy said, "Only those who dare to fail greatly can ever achieve greatly."

To help children embrace the process, encourage them to make mistakes! By purposefully doing something that seems against the rules and will possibly look like a mistake, you can help children discuss and explore *why* it didn't work, which enhances their knowledge of the activity or item—our ultimate goal. Help them to look beyond what they know and push past it.

For example, take a jar of water and pour it into a smaller jar. Keep pouring even when it begins to overflow. (Note: Creating a rule not to allow children to overfill jars would inhibit their stimulus freedom and opportunity for learning.) Obviously, the water will not fit into the smaller jar. But why? If water can fit in a jar, why wouldn't it fit in another jar?

What happened when you kept pouring? Where did the water go? Why? If you now pour the small jar of water back into the large jar, what happened? Where is all the water? Does it still exist? Can you get it back? You can see here how the activity can lead to a very in-depth discussion that involves lots of learning! All because of the mistake of spilling water.

An offshoot of making mistakes is the notion that there are right and wrong ways to do certain things. Howard Gardner (1993), director of Project Zero at the Harvard Graduate School of Education and the man who revolutionized our understanding of intelligence, said, "The key idea in the psychologist's conception of creativity has been *divergent thinking.* Intelligent people are thought of as convergers—people who, given some data or puzzle, can figure out the correct (or at any rate, conventional) response. In contrast, when given a stimulus or puzzle, creative people tend to come up with many different associations, at least some of which are idiosyncratic and possibly unique" (p. 20).

I have seen this in the children I teach. One in particular who comes to mind is a four-year-old named Ben. I had presented him with a set of sequence cards. There were four cards: one of a mother pouring juice into a cup for her daughter, one of the daughter picking up the glass, one of the daughter drinking the juice, and one of the empty cup sitting on the table. This was considered the "correct" sequence for the cards. When Ben placed them in order, he began with the one of the daughter picking up the glass, followed the "correct" sequence, but ended with the mother pouring the juice. I asked him to tell me the story to better understand his decision. He said, "There was a little girl who was thirsty and she started to drink some juice. She drank and drank and then it was gone, so she called her mommy and asked her to pour her more juice!"

While technically he got this task "wrong," it was obvious that his logic followed perfectly, and therefore I scored him as having done it right. This is an example of how standardized tests can often be unfair to creative children. Gardner (1993) points out that attempts to create standardized tests, akin to intelligence tests, have failed, mostly because they limit the creativity to a single industry or learning style (e.g., visual). Parents and teachers need to be advocates for their children's creativity and be careful that this creativity is not misinterpreted through standardized testing.

A study of a wide variety of classrooms found that approximately 90% of the questions asked by most teachers had only one right answer (Dacey & Packer, 1992). We need to teach our children that there are many right ways to answer.

Allowing for more than one right answer often goes against convention, and people who practice this are accused of doing it wrong. When we see people acting in a way that's different from the norm, we often see it as silly or ridiculous—even crazy. (Think of the Wright brothers when they told people they were going to fly.) However, I've always defined acting silly as "exhibiting unharnessed creativity." I crave creative moments, and when I don't get them often enough I tend to explode with them! And yes, it may look silly to a man for his grown wife to insist they play the sound-track from *Mary Poppins* while putting new siding on their house, even when the kids are not home. And yes, it probably looks ridiculous to a day care parent to walk in and see me standing on the couch with a pink boa around my neck and a cowboy hat on my head, throwing silk flowers into the air. And yes, even the kids look at me in shock when I spontaneously combust into a song about my bubble gum losing its flavor on the bedpost overnight while they are quietly doing puzzles. But each time, whether they want to admit it or not, they smile.

They smile, and they consider something they had never considered before. They open their minds to the possibility before them, and for that moment, creativity thrives. Then they begin to wonder what it would feel like to do that. Now admittedly, I don't think my husband said this to himself that day doing siding, but he's not known for his creativity anyhow (someone needs to be sane the majority of the time in our household, so he took the job). But the day care parents wonder, "Could I do something fun like that with my kids?" And the kids wonder, "Do you think I could sing *my* favorite song too when I do puzzles?" Unharnessed creativity begets creativity.

Many years ago, when I was very green at doing child care, I stumbled into a creativity workshop by Inez Learn (whom I mentioned earlier) just outside of Milwaukee, Wisconsin. When I walked out, I felt seven years old again and sat down to write a letter to my mother to thank her for teaching me all I ever really needed to know about raising kids that I had simply forgotten until that day. What Inez taught us was to stretch our minds, to wonder, to look at the world in a new way—to be creative. Almost every exercise she gave us, I quickly realized, was something that my own mother had done with us four girls when I was little. As I looked around the room, I saw women frantically taking notes, in awe of what they heard from her, seeing it all as a completely new idea. That's when I started my letter to Mom. None of it was new to me, but it had been forgotten. In the quest to grow up I had fallen into the biggest trap of all—I forgot what it was like to be a kid. Inez reminded me of the joy of a simple game, of the opportunity to create, of the power of imagination.

She gave us questions to stretch those creative muscles, to wake them up. Questions such as "Which is rougher: purple or green? Which is faster: a chain or a table? Which is heavier: an ocean or a mountain?" As adults we discount these types of questions as ridiculous and without answers.

Yet you ask children and they will *know* the answer. "Which is bigger: a pickle or a pain?" you ask. "A pain," says Megan. "I broke my arm last summer and it was bigger than anything in this world." But then, "A pickle," says Ben. "My grandma grows the hugest pickles you've ever seen and she gives me one each time I visit." They're both right. The answer changes for each person, but it's always right. It's about looking at something not as others see it, but as you see it. To not be influenced by the rules society puts on an object but to think beyond that, allowing your own point of view to be the guide—*that's* creativity. Even if it does sound silly to say that darkness is quicker than lightness. But it's true. Ask kids this question the next time they have to come inside from playing because it got dark outside. They'll tell you that the dark came very quickly but that it seems like morning will take a long time to come. Unharness their creativity and yours with these questions so that when someone accuses you of being silly you can answer, "Yes! Yes, I am!"

Another way to view this silliness is to see it as part of a greater whole. From these moments of creativity new ideas spring. Those new ideas then move into actions and ultimately become something of concrete value. Jean Piaget, the noted philosopher and developmental psychologist, described the stages of child development to be on a pendulum. Children grow so quickly they go from balanced to a state of disequilibrium and back. Begin to see the moments of creative energy as the period of disequilibrium, knowing that in the end it contributes to a balance in the child's development and learning.

The idea of supporting a child in bending the rules can often make adults worry that disciplinary problems may arise. They feel the need to implement rules, to safeguard their children. But rules take the decision-making process away from the child. So how can we protect our children while supporting their decision-making capabilities? It's about modeling what we are trying to teach our children, that the *process* is what matters. This means that rather than setting rules, parents and teachers who support a child's creativity will create limits but emphasize the *reasons* these limits are in place. This teaches children to think through situations, to evaluate how it will affect them and in the end, make their own decisions. It involves discussing the implications of certain behavior so children are in charge of finding their own solutions.

Identifying the limit to a particular behavior, and discussing the reasons the limit is where it is, opens the discussion to reexploration as the circumstances for the limit change, teaching the child that these circumstances are what is important in the decision-making process. For example, on a very cold day you may talk with your children about limiting their sledding to just three hours that afternoon because of the wind chill and possibility of getting sick or too cold. This is opposed to a rule that says they can sled for only three hours. The difference lies in the discussion about the reasoning. For if the next weekend the weather is warmer, the children will now understand that because the threat of the cold is no longer so high, they could now decide to sled for four hours and not find opposition. However, if the previous week a rule was imposed, the children would more likely sled for only three hours and not question the decision or build their understanding of it. They also would not learn to trust their instincts when being outside and have no basis for making a future decision on the length of time to be outdoors. By providing the limit with an explanation of the reason, it teaches the children to understand the important aspects of the decision so when faced with the same circumstances again, they will be able to make a good decision based on the new facts.

A classroom example of this is a rule limiting the time children can play in specific areas of the room. This is often done to maintain classroom management and allow children time to fully explore the areas they are in without it becoming crowded. But consider it from this point of view: By putting the focus on time without addressing the real issue (overcrowding), the children simply follow the rule but do not build an understanding of it. However, teachers can include children in discussions about overcrowding and let them help determine an optimal number of children in an area in order for them to play freely. Then children will be able to make their own decisions to move about based on the changing circumstance of the number of children in the area rather than the time rule.

Allowing children to feel free of the constraints of a particular setting or activity encourages their imagination and sense of creativity. The freedom will allow them to better understand why rules exist and to then use that knowledge to implement the concept in other areas of learning. Supporting unharnessed creativity, and even a little silliness now and then, helps children to think outside the box, to put new ideas together that they previously saw as separated, and to come to a new level of understanding to support all their other learning.

———————— ✦ ————————

Alexis had crawled onto the couch and started to jump. I said, "No jumping on the couch." She looked at me with an angelic smile and said, "We could hop!"

DELAYED GRATIFICATION

Delay of gratification is one of the more difficult traits for children of this new generation. We live in a world that moves faster and faster, that provides information with the click of a mouse, where you can buy, sell, explore, ask questions, get answers, and more in only moments. Children today want it all, and they want it *now*.

This desire to be instantly gratified creates a loss of patience. Without patience, it is nearly impossible for a scientist to finish an experiment, for an artist to finish a painting, or for an explorer to make it to the top of a mountain. Understanding that there are many processes in which time is needed in order to accomplish a positive outcome is a trait quickly disappearing in our youth—and therefore in desperate need of attention by parents and teachers alike.

Growing up, many of us heard our mothers say, "Good things come to those who wait!" We were taught that waiting is a part of life, that it would be worthwhile in the end. The Dr. Seuss (1990) book that is often given to graduates, *Oh, the Places You'll Go!*, commits an entire section to "The Waiting Place"—reminding children that waiting is a part of life, but then moving forward and showing that after the waiting good things will come, "you'll find the bright places where Boom Bands are playing" (p. 26).

Teachers often find resources that include what they call "transition activities." These activities are designed to make transitions—the waiting period between activities—go more smoothly and interestingly for children. These activities promote the idea that waiting is a negative thing and that time spent waiting should instead be filled with something present and interesting. Rather than teaching our children patience, we teach them to fill every moment of their time with an activity!

Imagine an adult's day where waiting was replaced with activity. People in elevators singing songs, people at vending machines reciting their agenda for the day while waiting for their coffee, a baker doing push-ups while waiting for a cake to bake! In many ways, we do see this today. People are texting messages while in the elevator and talking on the phone while waiting for coffee. Many people read the paper or a book while waiting for appointments.

I'm not suggesting we teach our children to sit quietly in every situation and do nothing. But there needs to be a balance between being bored and removing waiting from our list of important activities. Waiting can sometimes be a very exciting thing. We need to embrace the moments where waiting occurs in anticipation of something great and encourage this sense of excitement in our children. These are the moments when our creativity can thrive.

When we are waiting for results, we have the opportunity to explore the options the results may bring. While waiting for a cake to bake, we can talk about how high we think it will rise, whether or not we think the middle will be done, or the sides too brown, or if it will stick in the pan. It is a time to elicit a sense of wonder in children. Daydreaming is the perfect "transition activity."

Baking is an ideal opportunity to teach the value of delayed gratification. If you take the cake out because you don't want to wait, it will be runny! You *must* wait in order to get the yummy result. Abruptly ending an activity without waiting for the expected result, and seeing how by waiting we are rewarded, are excellent opportunities for our children to learn from.

Waiting is a part of life. It cannot be skipped or ignored. And in many cases, it *will* be worth the wait. To enhance our children's sense of creativity, they need the tools to stick it out, to follow their imaginations where they may go, and to take the time to see how it all turns out.

BALANCED-BRAIN THINKING

Balanced-brain activity is what brings together all the aspects of the previous three traits, using creative thinking to produce concrete output. It's what supports problem solving, a major component of all developmental learning, and underlines the importance of the three Cs.

Whenever you encourage the journey for children, you are offering them an opportunity to learn problem solving. Problem solving is often separated on early learning standards lists as its own standard and developmental milestone. Sometimes it comes under the heading of creativity; other times as a cognitive activity. The reason it appears in a variety of areas in state standards is because it is the *result* of specific learning in a couple of different areas rather than a specific area of learning itself. To problem solve is to consider the possibilities, analyze the effectiveness of each possibility, and come to a successful conclusion by choice. That means a child must first have the creative ability to consider possible solutions to a problem, then have the curiosity to explore these possibilities closely and analyze them, then have the self-esteem (and support system of others, aka "courtesy") to choose an answer and follow it through. Because all the three Cs underline the process of problem solving, there will be activities in each chapter that aid in supporting this process, rather than listing "problem solving" as stand-alone activities under only one standard. All the three Cs support problem solving—creativity is only the beginning!

Dacey and Packer (1992) state, "Creativity requires more than just imagination. It also requires accuracy, analysis and objectivity" (p. 90). The assumption is often made that creative people are right-brain thinkers, but the truth is that creative thinking comes from using both sides of the brain in unison. Divergent thinking is done in the right brain—we think imaginatively to find all the possible solutions. Then convergent thinking is done in the left brain—we now think critically in order to narrow down the possibilities. This is the basis for problem solving. It ties together creativity and curiosity—creativity in thinking of new ideas, curiosity in testing these ideas to see how they work. Both are necessary for any real action. The initial creative thought is a right-brain activity, but the curiosity to find what will actually work and what will not in order to solve the problem is a left-brain activity. In other words, to teach problem solving to children means to offer them opportunities for balanced-brain activities.

Supporting growth in the connections between the right and left brains builds creativity. However, this does not mean throwing the ridiculous out there for our children, bombarding them with stimulation to try to make these connections occur. Dacey and Packer (1992) warn that "stimulation must be *distinctive* and *meaningful* to promote cognitive growth" (p. 93). For example, a child in a family that is large and full of constant overlapping conversations, while seemingly a pool of verbal influence, because of its lack of one-to-one interaction may actually lead to poor verbal skills in the child. On the other hand, a small family with much less ongoing conversation taking place but a higher level of one-to-one discussions could support a higher verbal ability for a child. The quality of stimulation, rather than the quantity, makes the difference.

Creative activities, whether stand-alone or as stepping-stones to further learning, need to have a sense of quality, a reason for the child to engage and grow. Many children seek out this reason in their learning; a common question at school is, "Why do I need to know this?" Too often, educators do not have a solid reason other than it is in their curriculum, and therefore it must be important. By using creativity as a support for further learning, we are able to find the ways to make it important to the child. It opens doors for a new way to look at the information—a way that the child will have an interest in.

Teachers and parents can use what excites children, and allow them creative freedom to apply these topics to other areas of learning. Children who are not interested in math do not understand its importance in their lives. They will better appreciate it when they learn that in order for them to achieve success in the game of basketball they love, they will need to understand how the scoring works—what value a basket holds, how those values are added together, and how the comparison of the two totals determines the winner. In this way, the teacher and parent can make math relevant to these children.

Two areas that excite most children, and that are perfect for bringing balanced-brain learning into their day, are music and movement. Adding these activities into your daily routine may be a teacher or parent's secret to instilling not only balanced-brain activity but a surge of development in a variety of areas. *The Creative Curriculum for Preschool* states, "Music and movement experiences help develop both sides of the brain—an important finding in recent brain research—and contribute to children's social/emotional, physical, cognitive and language development" (Dodge, Colker, & Heroman, 2002, p. 423).

Music stimulates the right side of the brain, and movement stimulates the left side. By putting the two together, children not only have fun but get a balanced-brain workout. When you add information from other areas of learning, the activity explodes with possibilities for their development.

At Sam Houston State University, researchers studied the effects of early music training on intelligence. They found that the magnitude of improvement in abstract reasoning was proportional to the level of participation in the music curriculum. The children whose parents met "satisfactory" compliance standards for participation in the music activities jumped from the 50th percentile on standardized intelligence tests to above the 87th percentile (Bilhartz, 1999).

Engaging children in music activities can range from the simple—asking children to sing their ABC's while clapping—to the complicated—having children hop to a song and stop when they hear words that rhyme. Or they move to a particular piece of music as if they were a particular animal. Mix together your learning objectives with a piece of music and some body movements and you'll have a recipe for success.

Balanced-brain thinking is the basis for problem solving; it is an essential tool for children in their journey to further learning. Understanding that problem solving is more than one activity—it is actually three—gives parents and teachers the opportunity to support each of its components and to truly support a child's ability to problem solve. Supporting creative thought is only the beginning, but it is a necessary first step. Helping children to take this first step and carry it over to the next—exploring the possibilities (curiosity)—then following it through with a decision and action is a winning plan for any team.

These first four traits are thought processes that we can support through activities we offer. However, equally important is how we support these traits through our own attitudes and reactions to a child's creativity. The combination of providing activities to support creativity and an emotional atmosphere to support creative action sets the stage for success for every child.

We want our children to be original—to have the confidence to be different, to express their creativity. To have self-control—to be able to control their emotions and move forward. To have passion—a drive to get to the answer. To have tolerance of ambiguity—staying open-minded rather than give up when information is unknown. To not fear problem solving—to not worry when faced with a problem but simply see it as something to figure out.

All these traits come from self-confidence, and self-confidence comes from the experience of expressing oneself and feeling supported by those around you when you do. As we support our children's creative thinking, we want to also support their sense of self-confidence. This self-confidence will foster the responsibility and drive to tackle a problem, explore its options openly and uninhibitedly, and put together what is gathered in this process to come to a solution. We don't want our children just to have creative thoughts; we want to teach them they can *do* something with those ideas!

For educators and parents, this means not only providing the environment and stimulus for creative thinking but being prepared to allow children to follow through on their ideas, to share them with others, to act on them. For example, a boy comes to you and asks permission to build a fort in the backyard or school playground. You hand over items (both the obvious and unusual) such as a sheet, some brooms, a bucket, a stack of books, a ball of string, scissors, some scarves, paper and pencils, a couple of pots and bowls, and a box.

He gets to work outside, and before long he has erected a structure of sorts. He gleefully runs to you and asks you to come inside the fort and check it out. Rule 1: You do. Once inside, he begins to explain to you he has constructed a lookout station for deer. He shows you how he has cut a hole in the sheet to create a window and placed a box below it with paper and pencils for recording what he sees. He filled a bowl with berries he found and placed it outside the window to entice the deer. Then he asks, "Can I get some of my friends to make a team to help me watch the deer?" Rule 2: The answer is yes.

What can make giving these answers difficult is the fact that your backyard or playground looks out over the parking lot of the local fire station downtown. The chance for a deer sighting is next to none. As adults, we race to the end and think that if we can't accomplish the goal then the journey should be abandoned. Rule 3: For kids, it's all about the journey.

When the boy has his friends or classmates over to join him, he's stepping into a role of responsibility and leadership. He's taking his ideas a step further and taking his learning a step further as well. He may organize the group, hand out jobs, provide new props for them to use as tools, and give instructions he can only imagine. Soon all your props have a useful function and he is asking for more. After days of working in the deer observatory, it is likely he may come to the conclusion that you do not live in an area that deer like, so they will not be able to see one, but that perhaps next time he visits his grandma's farm he should build one there. But by coming to this conclusion on his own he has learned so much. He has learned that by pursuing his dreams, he will find answers. He has learned that he has the capabilities to find answers on his own without your help. He has learned to consider every aspect of the problem, continue to look for solutions, and persevere. It's not about the deer; it's about the journey.

Thinking creatively is an activity unto itself. It can occupy a self-driven child's mind for hours or even days. However, adults can also use creativity to open a path to learning that may otherwise be blocked for many children. Young ones who run the other way when asked to study writing or reading will be the first to the table when it comes under the umbrella of a creative activity. By adding creativity to developmental learning, you are providing the stepping-stone children need to reach their goals. Without it, many children struggle. It is such an integrated part of *how* they learn that to skip it would be like expecting them to climb on a roof without a ladder.

Think of creativity as the tool children need to get the job done. You won't nail down math without this particular hammer. Doing creative activities for the sake of fostering creativity is like practicing to hammer—you get the swing down and you gain control. Then you're ready when that nail comes along. You present children with math, put that hammer in their hands, and in one fell swoop—*bang!*—they've got it.

The biggest trick for teachers and parents is to find the right hammer. Creativity involves getting excited about something and pursuing it in many different ways. In a discussion of the research literature pertaining to a child's learning process, Solomon (2003) shares how knowledge of a particular topic can increase our interest and encourage a search for more knowledge of this topic: "Increased interest results in more effective knowledge construction" (p. 74).

The paths you take will likely be different for each child. In today's educational world, this is often a problem. Large classrooms and staff shortages lead to many large group activities that appeal to only a few in the group. Little time is spent one-on-one, which is necessary to help children find the inspiration they need to get started. Where parents and teachers can help each other is in discussing the individual child, what his or her interests are, what gets the child excited, and what doesn't. By sharing this information, it is possible even with a full classroom to identify several factors that would appeal to the individuals and, as a whole, get them on their way.

For example, in a preschool group of eight children, the teachers and parents may identify that three really love dinosaurs, two live to be princesses, two wish they could fly planes, and one would love to be in a plane that went back in time to find dinosaurs. When it came time to talk about math, the teacher could create three learning stations from these three broad topics and find creative ways to explore the math through those topics. It would engage the children's interest—give them that reason—support their creativity, and teach math. That's what this book is designed to do: Take what excites the kids, use it to tap into their creative side, and lead them to further learning.

Believe it or not, you can learn to be creative. All it takes is the ability to take a chance. Break the rules or bend them. Try something new. We were all born with creativity in us, but unfortunately, not all of us continued to practice it or experienced support of it by the adults in our lives. That doesn't mean we've lost the ability to be creative, but it means we have the power to help our children retain it for life. Start exercising your creative muscles again—give it a try! Stand on a chair and sing "Jailhouse Rock" at the top of your lungs. Stick your face in a ball of Play-Doh to see what impression it makes. Fill your sensory table or a plastic bin with mud. Wear your clothes backward and pretend they are just fine. Go out the window instead of the door. Teach your kids that as long as they are safe there is no "wrong" way to do things, some just more useful or imaginative than others. You've got to try them before you'll know!

Being a role model for children is key in opening their imaginations and sense of creativity. Albert Einstein tells us that "setting an example is not the main means of influencing others; it is the only means" (cited in Carlson, 2008, p. 11).

Role models from pop culture or history also help children to recognize creativity. Educators can provide books and other information on famous role models such as Pablo Picasso, Pete Rose, Magic Johnson, Abraham Lincoln, Walt Disney, Henry Ford, Dustin Hoffman, and Will Smith. Famous people from a variety of fields exhibit creativity that can inspire both children and adults.

To get your creative juices flowing, try reading *Inspiration Sandwich* by Sark (1992). Berkeley, CA: Celestial Arts.

The following two chapters will give you examples on just how to get them stretching those creative muscles. First, we'll explore activities that foster creativity as stand-alone activities. Next, we'll consider some of the developmental areas that appear in many standards of learning for states across our nation. It is unfortunate that the majority of these

Children's Books That Spark Creativity

Amelia Bedelia by Peggy Parish, illustrated by Fritz Siebel (1993). New York: HarperCollins.

Chicka Chicka Boom Boom by Bill Martin Jr. and John Archambault, illustrated by Lois Ehlert (1989). New York: Simon & Schuster.

The Patty Cake Kids and the Lost Imagination Cap by Patricia Dischler, illustrated by Ashly Kircher (2007). Madison, WI: Goblin Fern.

Stone Soup by Marcia Brown (1947). New York: Charles Scribner's Sons.

Swimmy by Leo Lionni (1963). New York: Random House.

standards do not include activities to foster creativity beyond exploring the arts. However, there are some that do. For those that do not, teachers can use the activities in this chapter to integrate creativity into other learning areas. For those who already have standards for creative learning, these activities will help you to meet those standards. When creativity is added to the curriculum, the support structure for learning is in place and children no longer struggle to reach their goals—you've given them the ladder to get there.

NOTE

1. From notes I took at her 1993 workshop in Milwaukee titled "Freeing Creativity in Children." I attended the same workshop a few other times over the years and I used ideas from her workshops often; she was very inspiring.

Creativity Activities 2

Increasing children's ability to be creative can be done as easily as increasing their ability to do math or play music—practice, practice, practice. There are certain brain functions that support creative thought, so by "stretching" those particular muscles, we help children become stronger in those areas. Functional freedom, stimulus freedom, delayed gratification, and balanced-brain thinking can be practiced. The following activities will help you and the children unleash your creative potential.

FUNCTIONAL FREEDOM

When children realize that they can use items in unconventional ways, they open the door to creative thinking. Encourage them to see things in a new way, to combine uncommon things into new sets, to explore as they never have before. Freedom from preconceived ideas is the foundation of creative thinking. All of the activities in this chapter meet state standards for cognitive development.

CRITTER SCHOOL

Critter (worm, cricket, beetle, ant, etc.)

Habitat (pan or box with soil)

Bell

Hairdryer (to be used by an adult)

Place the critter on the habitat. When the child rings the bell, the adult blows low heat onto the critter. The critter will dig down into the soil to avoid the warm air. After doing this several times, the critter will dig down just from hearing the bell. *Seeing that even these small critters can learn cause and effect and essentially be "trained" by it will broaden a child's view of insects as pests and establish functional freedom. Note: This activity can be used to introduce a learning session about insects.*

LOOK WHAT ELSE I CAN DO!

Provide a basket with several items in it, have the children explore each one, and discuss how many uses they can think of for each—for example, peanut butter as sunscreen! Possible items: candle, socks with holes, sponge, hammer, peanut butter, bar of soap. *This activity encourages functional freedom by exploring uses that are not typical for the item.*

BOOK BLOCKS

Provide children with a large pile of books of a variety of sizes and shapes. Try to gather books that range from very small board books to large encyclopedia-type books. Ask the children to build something from the books as if they were using building blocks. They are allowed to open the books to create roofs, corners, and so on. When they are finished, give them materials to draw what they created. If they are writing, have them add a title and a short paragraph telling a story about what they built. *This activity supports creativity through functional freedom in building with books.*

PLANTS ARE DYING

Engage in a discussion of plants and vegetables and their uses. Then stretch those ideas by introducing the use of the plants and veggies as dye. Adults can boil the items (different plants or veggies in each batch), let the mixture cool, then present it to the children along with cloth items such as old tee shirts or towels (cotton works best). Have them discuss what was boiled and if they think it will dye the clothing and, if so, what color. Soak items and watch to see what works and what doesn't. Talk about why you think some items got dyed and others didn't. After the activity, advance the discussion by asking what other uses they can now find for the dyed items. *Activity supports creativity through use of plants and vegetables as dye.*

REINVENTING THE WHEEL

Have the children pick a favorite item—a bike, CD player, or toy—and think of ways it could be made even better. Provide pencils and paper for them to draw their new inventions—for example, a glow-in-the-dark bike for riding at night. Then have the children invent items to do things they need. Help them to think of problems they face, such as believing there are monsters under their bed, and what they can invent to help solve it, such as a periscope that bends to look under the bed. Have them draw their ideas or make models from clay or other materials. *Activity supports creativity as children think beyond what they know and become inventive.*

CRAZY TABLE SETTINGS

Have the children think of nontraditional items to set the table with for a meal, such as tee shirts for placemats, Frisbees for plates, clothespins to pick up food, and so on. Encourage the outlandish and crazy! *Activity supports functional freedom as children consider nontraditional place-setting items.*

BE A MODEL OF IMPERFECTION

Model for your child how items can have alternate uses than what they were originally intended for, such as using a can to roll your cookie dough, putting pennies in a sock for a paperweight, and using a boot as a bookend. *Activity supports creativity through functional freedom and adult modeling.*

SCAVENGER HUNT

Send your child on a hunt for five things in your house or school that can all be used to do the same thing. Examples include using a vase or a horn to hold a flower, using a pen or a berry to write on paper, and using a chair or a stack of books to sit on. You can provide the theme (such as things you can write with) to help them get started, but allow some time for them to discover their own matches. *Activity encourages a creative look at items and their functions.*

HOUSTON, WE HAVE A PROBLEM!

Set up a dramatic play situation for the children (any theme will work) and allow them a day to explore it. On the second day, remove an item that you had observed as being central to their play the day before. Tell the children, "We have a problem! The _____ is no longer here; what could we use instead?" Be open to their suggestions and support them by providing the materials they feel are necessary to re-create the missing item. Or you could offer them a "toolbox" that contains an assortment of odd items they can choose from to create what they need. Allow their sense of creativity to guide them through the trial and error of finding their own solution. Encourage their sense of flexibility in situations that pose the unexpected. *Activity supports creativity through functional freedom as children problem solve for a replacement item.*

STIMULUS FREEDOM

Creative children are unafraid of bending the rules, and they see rules as aids in their actions. They don't assume there *are* rules. "I can't" is typically not a phrase they will use. Instead, it is "I'll try." Showing children that rules are meant to be guidelines but that they can look past them and see the world in new ways will support their creative thinking. In addition, changing their environment can help them change their thinking and support stimulus freedom. Many famous writers and artists insist on a specific environment to work in because they feel it best supports their creative thinking. I wrote most of this book while listening to big band music and bouncing on my exercise ball at my desk in my bright purple office (*my* creative environment)! Use your environment and the items in it to stimulate children's thought processes.

STORY TIME

Change the location of your story time—read a book under the table, outside sitting on top of the picnic table, lying down on your back in a pile of leaves, or standing in a circle. Notice how the different locations affect how the children react to the story. Each time, ask them how they feel and discuss what feels the best for them. *Activity supports stimulus freedom as children consider the effects of a variety of locations.*

SING! SING! SING!

Have a singing day. Instead of talking with the children in your regular tone of voice—sing! Sing "Good Morning," sing their storybook, sing instructions, and sing everything else you would have said normally throughout the day. By modeling this behavior, you are teaching the children stimulus freedom and encouraging them to try new behaviors in expected settings. Watch and see which children join in—or perhaps, which choose a different mode of "talking" for the day, such as whispering, yelling, or monotone. *Activity supports stimulus freedom as children experience, through your modeling, a new approach to each day.*

BACKYARD STEW

Bring a large cooking pot outdoors and fill it half full with water. Ask the children to make you some stew using things they find outdoors: berries, leaves, moss, dirt, and so on. Give them a large spoon to stir it up. Bring other kitchen items outdoors to add to the cooking experience. *Activity provides stimulus freedom as items from both inside and out merge during play.*

INSPIRING PLACES

Provide children with different types of areas of play. Give them a small, dark fort such as a box, or a closet for them to sit inside of with the door removed and a shimmering curtain hung up instead. Have places with hard surfaces and soft, with tall ceilings and low, all one color or with lots of color. See how different children react in each space. Have them draw pictures while in the spaces. Change spaces and ask them to draw again. Have them share the pictures and how they felt in each place they were drawing and how they think it affected their drawing. *Activity supports creativity through a variety of environmental stimulation.*

ALPHABET FAMILIES

Give your children four-inch cutouts of their first initials. Use heavy paper. Then provide other items and have them turn the letters into people or animals by gluing, painting, or drawing on them. Note: This can be combined with learning letters in that you are teaching them that letters represent *something*. During this activity, they represent people or animals, and during reading activities, they represent sounds. *Activity supports stimulus freedom as children change letters into people.*

UPSIDE-DOWN WORLD

Lay with your child on the floor or on a couch with your back on the seat and your feet facing up to the ceiling. Discuss the way the room looks now that it is upside down. Talk through a walk around—"Don't forget to step around the light!" "The window is so close to the floor now!" *Activity supports stimulus freedom as children are provided an alternate view and perception of their environment.*

SIMPLY AMAZING

Draw a very simple picture for the child, like a square and a circle, or a stick person and a flower. Then ask the child to create a fantastic story about something crazy or wild to go with the picture. *Activity supports creativity as children use their imaginations to see the possibilities beyond the simple object or shape they see.*

FAVORITE STORY REWRITE

Read a favorite story with your child. Then close the book and have the child retell the story, adding twists. For example, maybe the prince should ride a cow instead of a horse! Or change who the "winner" is in the storyline. Add dinosaurs or a rainfall of flower petals. Encourage creativity in the activity through modeling—tell your own version as well. *Activity supports stimulus freedom as children see they can change stories.*

A SQUARE IS NOT JUST A SQUARE

Give your children colored paper to cut into various shapes of their liking. They can be circles, squares, and so on, but they can also be squiggles and other odd shapes. Then give them glue and markers and have them paste them onto a larger sheet of paper to make something new—maybe an animal, person, house, or scene. *Activity supports stimulus freedom as children consider shapes as only parts of a whole rather than an end result.*

IT'S NOT WHAT YOU SEE, IT'S WHAT YOU *DON'T* SEE THAT COUNTS

Using a pencil, shade a large area of a sheet of paper. Provide the child with an eraser and ask him or her to erase what does *not* belong in the picture. Help the child to understand the power of negative space. This is not "drawing" with the eraser but, rather, looking at the pencil shading, seeing a picture in it, then erasing the shading that doesn't belong there so that what is left is a picture made with the shading. This is how sculpting works—the artist removes the part of the stone or clay that is not part of the form they see inside it. *Activity supports stimulus freedom as it looks at drawing through a different perspective than is typical.*

DELAYED GRATIFICATION

Learning that time can affect outcomes is an important aspect of creativity. Children can use this knowledge when being creative. For example, when given the challenge of finding different ways to lighten the color of a piece of material, while others are using bleach, a creative child will put the material in the sun and wait a week.

TIME IN A BOTTLE

Have your children collect items that are important to them now. Place them in a shoe box–sized plastic bin and bury it in the yard. Dig it up in six months or a year. Discuss how life has changed, how what is important to them has changed, how it felt to wait to see the items again. The wait becomes part of the process. If you had dug up the items the next day, it would have taken away from the excitement and discovery. Chances are, nothing would have changed for the children yet. Show them how waiting is an important part of letting life evolve and change. *Activity supports delayed gratification and teaches children the value that time adds to items.*

LEAVING ONE STONE UNTURNED

Help the children find a large rock; place it in a flowerbed or in the woods. First note how the ground looks before putting it down. Leave it for one month. Don't let the children peek under! Teach them to wait—it will be worth it. They can look at it but not touch it. After one month, let them turn it over and they may see a new family of insects living underneath. *Activity supports delayed gratification as children wait and see the change that time brings to a simple act.*

SQUISHY ART

Provide the children two large sheets of paper each. Have them put on paint smocks and sit at the table. Place the first paper down, then squirt two to three different colors of paint on the paper. Place the second paper on top. Tell the children to use their hands to squish the paint around on top of the paper. Tell them not to lift the top paper to see what is happening. Give them a good amount of time to squish the paint—five minutes at least. Delay the unveiling a bit longer by asking the children to first guess what their pictures look like. If they had two colors (e.g., blue and yellow), after squishing what color would they also have? Ask them to use their fingertips to "write" their names on the top paper. Ask them if they think it will appear in the paint on the bottom paper. After discussions, finally allow the children to unveil their squishy art—one at a time! Help children to value the process and the activity and become more comfortable with the wait. *Activity supports delayed gratification as children participate in an activity but wait for the result.*

PAPIER-MÂCHÉ EGGS

Making papier-mâché projects is a great delay-of-gratification project—they take six days to make but are wonderful when finished. An egg is the simplest shape to make. They can be small or large and can be made for a unit on farm animals (chickens), Easter, dinosaurs, birds, or even cooking.

Start with a round balloon, blowing it up to the size you would like the egg to be. Note: Larger is actually easier because you don't have to try to get the paper strips to bend as much around the shape. Have the children help you tear newspaper into long strips depending on the size of your egg shape. The strips should be approximately half the length of the egg shape and one inch wide. Make a mixture of equal parts white glue and water. Secure the balloon by taping the knotted end to a block or other heavy object. Dip the pieces of newspaper into the glue mixture and lay them onto the balloon. Overlap the strips until the balloon is covered. Do just one layer of paper at first. Let dry overnight. Repeat the process, adding a second layer. Dry overnight again.

Remove the balloon from the block and use a pin to pop the balloon. Shake the balloon out if desired or leave it in for a slight rattle. Turn the egg upside down and add paper strips dipped in glue mixture in order to cover the hole. Dry overnight. Sit the egg into a cup to hold it upright and have the child paint the top half however appropriate for the theme you are using (bright stripes for an Easter egg, brown and green spots for a dinosaur egg, white for a chicken egg, blue for a robin egg, etc.). Dry overnight. Turn the egg over and place in the cup again to paint the other half. Dry overnight. Day six arrives and it's finally done! But it will definitely be worth the wait as the children enjoy their egg creations. *Activity supports delayed gratification as children learn to follow time-consuming steps in order to reach the result.*

HELP ME, I'M MELTING!

After a winter snow, have the children build small snowmen—three balls, each about four inches in diameter. Place their tiny snowmen in bowls and bring them inside. They can decorate the snowmen using baby carrots and raisins. Have each child guess how many hours it will take for his or her snowman to melt and put the number on a card in front of the child's bowl. Check the snowmen throughout the day, taking note of what time each melts and who was closest to their predicted time. In addition to the delayed gratification, this is a great opportunity to show the children the dirt now floating in the water. If you live in an area that doesn't have snow, you can make some using ice cubes and a blender. Chop up the ice as you would to make a lemon ice. Give it to the children in a large bowl to scoop up and make their snowballs. *Activity supports creativity as children consider the possibilities, and delayed gratification as they wait to see the outcomes.*

EGG HEADS

Start collecting eggshells when cooking. Try to break them at the tip, leaving at least half, or closer to ¾, of the eggshell intact. Wash them thoroughly with warm, soapy water and let dry overnight. Give each child an egg, some potting soil, and some grass seed. Have the children sit their eggs in shallow cups (such as bathroom paper cups) or in drink bottle lids. Using permanent markers, have the children draw a face on their eggs. Fill half full with potting soil, then sprinkle with grass seed. Water with a spray bottle, squirting a few times. Put in a sunny window and water each morning. After a few days, the grass will begin to grow and in a week to two weeks their eggs will have grown "hair"! They can trim it as it grows. *Activity supports delayed gratification as children wait for the grass to grow and are rewarded with the results.*

ICE BLOCKS

Create some blocks that are completely out of the ordinary—make ice blocks! Gather lots of different shapes of containers, such as plastic storage containers in squares, rectangles, bowl shapes, in large and small sizes, as well as pie plates, cake pans, muffin tins—almost any shape that can hold water will work. If you live in an area that gets cold outside, place the containers outside, fill them with water (kids can do this using a water pitcher), then add food coloring to each, making lots of different colors. Stir with a spoon to distribute the coloring. If you can't freeze them outside, use a regular freezer. Freeze overnight. The next day, you can remove the various "blocks" for the children to build with outside—whether it is warm or cold, this will be loads of fun! If it's cold, the structures they build will freeze together solid overnight; if it's warm, they will melt. For added fun in the warm weather areas, build the structure on a white sheet or towel. When it melts overnight, the food coloring will leave a cool design. (Also, it makes losing the structure not so bad anymore.) *Activity supports delayed gratification as children wait for the ice blocks to form.*

RAIN, RAIN, DON'T GO AWAY!

When you are expecting lots of rain, place a measuring cup or a rain gauge outside where the children can check on it. Have them collectively agree on how much it will rain. Decide on a prize if it reaches this amount, such as a special game or toy they can play with, or a treat. Check often during the day to see if the rain is getting close to the mark. When it reaches the mark, celebrate together! *Activity supports delayed gratification as children wait for the rain level to rise and are rewarded for their wait.*

ABSTRACT ART NAMES

Give the children a sheet of white paper each. Then give them colored markers for each letter in their names. Have them put on blindfolds and draw the first letter of their names on the paper, large enough to fill it. Have them continue with the other letters in their names, using a different color for each and keeping the blindfolds on. When they are done, they should have wonderful abstract pieces of art that represent the letters of their names in a fun and creative way. *Activity supports delayed gratification as children create without seeing immediate results.*

YUMMY THINGS COME TO THOSE WHO WAIT!

Baking with yeast is a great delayed-gratification activity for children. First they make the dough; then they have to wait for it to rise, then punch it down and wait for it to rise again, and then they wait while it bakes! Lots of waiting, but a big payoff at the end. Here's a simple cinnamon roll recipe to use for this activity:

Cinnamon Rolls

½ cup water

½ cup milk

1 pkg. yeast

⅓ cup sugar

⅓ cup butter, melted

1 tsp. salt

½ tsp. vanilla

1 egg

3½ to 4 cups flour

1–2 Tbsp. oil

2 Tbsp. butter, melted

¼ cup sugar

2 tsp. cinnamon

Glaze

¼ cup butter, melted

4 Tbsp. hot water

½ tsp. vanilla

1½–2 cups powdered sugar

Heat milk and water together to 105–115 degrees. Add yeast and stir to dissolve. Stir in sugar, butter, salt, and vanilla. Mix in egg and two cups of the flour. Beat for a couple of minutes until smooth and light. Mix in enough of remaining flour, a little at a time, until smooth and easy to handle. Turn dough out onto floured surface to knead for about five minutes, until smooth and elastic. Oil a metal bowl. Place dough in bowl; turn over so oiled side is up. Cover with towel and let rise until doubled in size, about two hours. Punch down dough. Roll dough out on floured surface into a rectangle about 18 × 8 inches. Brush with melted butter. Mix together sugar and cinnamon. Sprinkle over dough. Starting at long side, roll dough up into a log. Cut log into 1½-inch sections. Place slightly apart in two greased cake pans, about six rolls to a pan (five around sides, one in center). Cover and let rise until doubled, about one hour. Bake in 375-degree oven for 25 minutes, until golden brown. Mix the first three glaze ingredients together, then add powdered sugar until smooth. Spread glaze while rolls are warm. *Activity supports delayed gratification as children bake, taking time to execute a time-consuming recipe.*

BALANCED-BRAIN THINKING

By combining problem-solving activities with sensory experiences, you are engaging both right- and left-brain thought processes—and expanding a child's capacity for creative thinking. Creative children will use all their senses to solve a problem, giving them important information that others may miss.

FRUIT FIND

Give each child an orange. Have the children examine their oranges closely using their sense of touch—where and how big the bumps and soft spots are, how large and heavy the orange feels, and so on. Then put all the oranges into a large paper bag. One at a time, and without looking, have the children reach in to try to find their oranges. Discuss how they were able to. Find other items to play this game with. *Activity supports balanced-brain activity as children use their sense of touch to consider the possibilities and then analyze these to find their oranges.*

PLAYING PICASSO

Place a simple drawing or photo on a lap tray with legs. Put a piece of paper on the table under the tray that the child can reach to draw on—but not see. Or place the drawing or photo on a table, put a chair under the table with the paper on it, and have the child stand next to the table. Do the same for each child. You want the drawing or photo to be seen, but not the paper. Ask the children to copy the drawing or photo. Encourage them to look closely, to match the movement of the pens with the outlines. Tell them to use their eyes as their pens and just let their pens follow. Go slowly. The drawing may look completely off balance—or it may be a perfect match! It is a great exercise for getting the mind and body to work together. *Activity supports balanced-brain activity as memory and motion work together.*

HOW MANY WAYS CAN WE GET TO THE MOON?

Engage children in a discussion of problem solving the many ways they could get to the moon. Let them know that they can use anything they wish, including new things that they invent or items they already have. Give a couple examples to get them going: "We could stack up all the lawn chairs of every person in our state and climb to the moon. Or we could build the biggest ball ever and sit on top of it as our friends fill it with air, and when it is completely filled, it will have lifted us all the way to the moon!" After coming up with many possibilities, move the discussion into choosing the one that would most likely work in reality. *Activity takes the children from right-brain thinking—considering all possibilities—to left-brain thinking—analysis and accuracy.*

SOUND BINGO

Create a sound bingo game, recording sounds around the classroom or on a trip to the zoo or a farm—wherever you can collect interesting sounds. Be sure to say the name of the sound a few seconds after recording it so you don't forget what it was. Then, using the Internet, find photos or drawings of the things you recorded to assemble into bingo boards. Play the recording for the children and give them bingo chips or small toys to mark the sounds they find, trying to get one full row in order to win. Have the children guess what the sound is before playing the answer; they can use the photos on their boards as clues to narrow down the possibilities. See if they agree with one another, or discuss the possibilities with the group. Then play the answer. *Activity supports balanced-brain function through the use of both sight and sound for matching.*

BLINDFOLD TASTE MATCHING

Blindfold a child sitting at a table and offer an item to taste. Then give three new items to taste and see if the child can pick the one that matches the first one. Examples would be pieces of pineapple, chocolate chip cookie, and apple. Choose one to be the matching piece as well. *Activity supports balanced-brain activity through sensory identification and matching.*

TRUCK FACTORY

Provide the children with a large appliance box and lots of additional props to use, such as paper towel tubes, paper plates, plastic cups, string, fabric, miscellaneous lids, pieces of construction paper, felt, yarn, paints, and so on. Have the children decide together what type of vehicle they would like to make, such as a fire truck, police car, ambulance, or school bus. Then allow them time and materials to make one. This is a project that can take a week or even more; give them a little time on it each day. As they hit roadblocks, provide photos of the real thing, books about it, and so forth, to give them new ideas. Also, be ready to get new props for them as they request items. Be there to support their project, but let the children's ideas drive the direction it goes. *Activity supports balanced-brain activity as children problem solve to create something with the box.*

WHAT'S UNDERGROUND?

Get the children curious about what is under the ground, and then find a place outside where they're allowed to dig in. Keep in mind that any spot dug up can be fixed when you're done with a little grass seed. Talk with the children about how they think they can dig the hole to see what is under there. Let them come up with a list of many things, such as a shovel, spoon, stick, backhoe, bowl, fingers, pie pan, and so on. Help them stretch their creative muscles as they think of things they could use to dig. Write down the full list. Then gather the items you are able to and give the children a chance to see how they work. Allow them a few days to work on the hole with the digging tools. After they get a foot or two down, spend some time talking about how the soil looks there and comparing it to how it looks at the top. Discuss which digging tool was the most effective. Expand into a math activity by having the dug-up dirt put into buckets and guessing how many buckets it will take to get a hole that measures 24 inches deep. *Activity supports balanced-brain activity through problem solving, analyzing the possibilities in order to make the best choice.*

COOKIE MADNESS

Make a batch of chocolate chip cookie dough, but don't put in the chocolate chips. Talk with the children about how this famous recipe was created because someone thought of combining two things they liked—cookies and chocolate. Ask the children to think of all the foods they like, encouraging them to name any of them, such as mashed potatoes, ham, carrots, peas, cucumbers, milk, cheese, and so on. Make a list. Gather the items. Spoon out one rounded teaspoon of the dough on a cookie sheet, then have each child add one favorite food item to the dough (if the item is large, cut in small bits), sprinkle bits of food over the dough and press in. Bake cookies at 350 degrees for 12 minutes. Have a tasting party to see if you've discovered the next new famous cookie! *Activity supports balanced-brain function as children use the sense of taste to explore possibilities.*

Integrating Creative Learning

3

Creativity is often separated in a state's list of early learning standards. Typically, it is touched on through standards related to art and problem solving. The following activities will help you to ensure it is an underlying concept in many other content areas. Research shows us that all learning is enhanced through integrated learning—the more we combine developmental areas of activities, the more successful each will be. By integrating creativity into all other areas of development, teachers and parents not only support creative development but also support advanced learning in every other developmental area. The following sections are standard areas of development seen in the early learning standards for many states. Activities that integrate creativity while also focusing on the early learning standard are listed in each area so that teachers and parents can find ways to not only meet their state standards for development but offer a program that supports the basis of learning potential as well—creativity. Note that all creative activities promote cognitive development, as it is intrinsic to creative thought processes, but in this chapter, creative activity is integrated into the other state standard areas.

LANGUAGE AND LITERACY

NAME BINGO

Write the letters of each child's name on index cards, one letter per card. To keep the game fair, the children need the same number of cards each, so you can use combinations of first and last names, add initials, or draw simple pictures of things they like. For example, if each child has six spaces to fill:

Amanda = A/M/N/D/L/H (initials for middle and last name added) You can either have just one space for *A*, or add in the other spaces for the *A*s in her name—but be sure there are six *different* squares to fill to keep it fair. When *A* is called, she can cover all the *A* squares.

Rachel = R/A/C/H/E/L

Sven = S/V/E/N/drawing of a cat/drawing of a dog (his pets)

Ben = B/E/N/S/A/M (Ben, plus the name of his best friend, Sam)

Write their letters and draw the pictures on a strip of paper with six blocks marked on it. Give the children small toys or bingo chips to cover the spaces. Mix the index cards together, and then draw them out of a box or bag one at a time and call them out. When one is called that matches one of their squares, they get to cover it. First one whose squares are all covered wins. Play several times so different children get a chance to win. *Activity supports delayed gratification as they wait to get all their letters while supporting literacy skills as they focus on recognizing the spoken and written versions of the letters in their names.*

SILLY SENTENCE

This activity helps children practice alliteration (words beginning with the same sound) as well as stretch their creative muscles and improve their memory. Create a silly sentence using alliteration. Then ask the children to repeat it. Make the sentence longer. Repeat again. Continue this for as long as you can add to the sentence. For older children, you can ask if they can think of words to add to the sentence. An example:

Silly Sally sings

Silly Sally sings songs

Silly Sally sings songs slowly

Silly Sally sings songs slowly so

Silly Sally sings songs slowly so Sam

Silly Sally sings songs slowly so Sam . . .

sings silly songs swiftly sending Silly Sally screaming!

Activity supports functional freedom as children explore words with a focus on the beginning sound rather than on how much sense the sentence makes while supporting literacy skills through the practice of alliteration.

DOWN BY THE BAY

This classic song is a perfect combination of imagination, rhyming practice, and musical rhythm. To stretch this as a literacy activity, after singing, allow the children to draw pictures of their favorite verse and write the verse for them at the bottom of the picture. A class songbook can then be created with them.

"Down by the Bay"

Down by the bay, where the watermelons grow,

Back to my home, I dare not go.

For if I do, my mother will say,

"Did you ever see a goose kissing a moose down by the bay?"

Refrains:

"Did you ever see a whale with a polka-dotted tail down by the bay?"

"Did you ever see a fly wearing a tie down by the bay?"

"Did you ever see a bear combing his hair down by the bay?"

"Did you ever see llamas eating their pajamas down by the bay?"

"Did you ever see a time when you couldn't make a rhyme down by the bay?"

You can also encourage the children to make up their own refrains, such as, "Did you ever see a bear braiding his hair down by the bay?" Provide the children the name of an animal, and then ask them to find the rhyming word to make the sentence. *Activity supports stimulus freedom through creative activities for animals to do while supporting literacy learning through rhyming practice.*

TAKE A TRIP TO SILLY CITIES

Line up with the children like a train; begin marching around the room, making chugging noises. When you stop, tell the children you are stopping at _____, and make up a silly name for a city, such as Purple Town or Jumping Frogs Junction. Ask the children to look out the train windows and tell you what colors they see, how it smells, if it is cold or hot, what the people are dressed like, and what they are eating or doing. Make at least three stops on your "trip." When done, ask each child to pick a favorite town and draw a picture of it. Then review, asking them what they saw in each city and writing it down. Put this all together to create a book, "Our Trip to Silly Cities," for the children to enjoy. *Activity combines (1) a creative experience of functional freedom in imagining a new place and noticing details in it and (2) literacy activities of writing about what they see and illustrating it.*

WHAT'S MY ENDING?

Choose a storybook for the children with a solid plot that poses a problem and a solution. Read the story to the children just up to the part where a solution is about to be revealed. Ask the children to then come up with their own endings to the story and share with the group. They can draw pictures to go along with them if they wish. Or rather than many different endings, the children can work together to find the ending, with each child providing one line, and then passing the story on to the next child to add another line. *Activity promotes (1) stimulus freedom by showing children they are not constrained by a prepublished storyline but have the power to change it at their will and (2) literacy skills as they learn to build a story. Activity also promotes curiosity as children explore all the possibilities for the ending.*

LET'S MAKE AN OINKALOPE!

In teaching literacy, we strive to help children understand that words represent things. To accomplish this, we show them words and match them to the items. However, we can accomplish this concept of *word = thing* while tossing in some creativity. Help the children to create their own "things." Start by writing down the name of an animal—*pig*, and then draw a picture of one next to it. Next, write down the sound the animal makes—*oink*. Next, choose another animal—*antelope*, write down its name, and draw its picture. Now combine the *sound* the first animal makes and the *last half* of the second animal's name and write the new word— *oinkalope*. At this point, have the children describe what they think an oinkalope would look like, where it would live, what it would do, what it would eat. *Activity builds on a basic lesson of literacy and expands it through functional freedom of creating new animals.*

BACKWARD BOOKS

Use a storybook that is familiar to the children, only this time, read the book from its end to its beginning! Children really enjoy the pure silliness of this activity. Next, read a storybook that is new to them. Read it backward as well. When done, ask the children if they can tell you the story—in the correct order, not backward. *Activity supports literacy learning through story, taking a twist to it to promote stimulus freedom by diverging from the stated rule or reading front to back, and then helping the children to reestablish the stated rule by putting it back in order at the end.*

STORY BAG

Create an interesting cloth bag using a bright print—perhaps with fun animals—or using brightly colored velvet. Add a gold drawstring. Make the bag very special. Fill it with small items such as a book, toy car, key, brush, doll, button, paper clip, spoon, ribbon, and so on. Gather the children at your circle time area, or settle in cozily with one child in a rocking chair, and tell them you are going to create a story together using the items in your Story Bag. Start by reaching in and pulling out one item. Begin the story with this item. Pass the bag to the next child and have him or her pull out an object and add to the story using the object. Continue until everyone has had a turn and the story is complete. Encourage the children to add silly things to the story such as, "One day a dolly was sitting on her bed. She began to brush her hair when all of a sudden a key dropped out of the sky and came through her window and landed on her bed. She tried to use the key to start a toy car but it didn't work. Then she used the key to open a book and all of the characters in the book came to life!" The story will change each time you play as they pull out items in a different order and they imagine new things happening. *Activity supports creativity through functional freedom as items are seen as parts of a story while supporting literacy through story building.*

HOW DOES A PIG TALK?

Next time you read a story, ask the children how they think the voice of each character sounds. Encourage them to be very silly with it, using very high or low voices or a growly voice. Let the children take turns being each character and repeating the line you say, but in the silly voice. Change as you read along, giving other children an opportunity to interpret the character's voice. Doing this helps stories come alive for children and gets them more involved. It teaches them storytelling skills and gets them actively thinking about characters beyond how the story presents them, using their imaginations to come up with the voices. For example, they may use a raspy voice and explain that the character has a sore throat today, even though it doesn't say so in the book. *Activity supports stimulus freedom as children look beyond the confines of the words in the book to become a part of the story and have a better understanding of the characters. It also supports literacy as children see how words in a story create an impression of a character.*

NURSERY RHYME MIX-UP

Write down lines from standard nursery rhymes on cards, one line per card. Put all of one nursery rhyme on cards of the same color; use a different color for each rhyme. Then put the cards into piles, one rhyme per pile. Pick them up and read the nursery rhyme. Then fan out the cards of one color and have a child pick one. Repeat for each of the other rhymes. It works best if you have a minimum of four. The children will now have one line each from each of four (or more) rhymes. Put these lines together on the table (or floor) for the children to see and read—you now have a completely new, silly poem! It most likely will not rhyme, but it will be fun to read. Discuss why it doesn't rhyme anymore; then work with the children to see how you can change it a bit so it does rhyme (but remains silly!). *Activity teaches (1) stimulus freedom as children no longer see rhymes as a set but as parts that can be changed and (2) literacy skills by creating new rhymes.*

MATH

BAKING MATH

Any recipe is a great opportunity for math. Measuring especially should be fully explored. For example, if the recipe calls for one cup of flour, ask the children to figure out how many half cups that is, or a mix of ¼ cups and ⅛ cups. Break down the amounts and help the children build up to the appropriate amount. There are other math opportunities—cutting cookies into various shapes, cutting a pie into eight or six slices, or counting the chocolate chips you'll put in, guessing before you count how many there will be. *Baking activities not only are full of math experiences (and science), they support creative growth because of the delay in gratification. Waiting for the finished product teaches children to look beyond the immediate and see value in the future.*

CLASSIFICATION CLEANING

At the end of the day, rather than asking the children to clean the room and put items away where they typically belong, have them create new classifications for the items and create new ways to store them. For example, they may decide to take all the blue toys and put them together on a shelf or in a bin. Or all the wooden toys or plastic toys must be together. They may decide all the small items can go together and all the big items should line up against a wall. Guide children toward breaking past the standards to see new commonalities among items in the room and reclassify them. *Activity combines math classification and stimulus freedom, going past the normal rules of the classroom to discover something new.*

PREDICTABLE PLAYMATES

Using a large sheet of paper or a chalkboard, create a graph listing all the children's names down one side and different questions along the top. Introduce a question and ask each child to guess how many of the children in the group will answer yes to the question. Write their guesses in the column next to that child's name. Possible questions include "Do you have a cat?" "Do you live on a farm?" "Do you go to ballet?" "Do you like to play baseball?" After the children's guesses are recorded, have the children who can answer yes to the question raise their hands; then count them, recording the number in a final row under the names. Discuss who guessed right or how close they were. Together, count how many guesses each child was off from the actual total. *Activity supports balanced-brain thinking by engaging children in the prediction process, a right-brain activity, while supporting mathematical learning through counting, graphing, and number comparisons, a left-brain activity.*

BODY NUMBERS

Show the children how to use their bodies to make numbers. Standing straight for number one. Curving a hand over your head while kneeling for number two. Kneeling with an arm over the head and an arm bent out from the waist for number three. Once the children get the idea, let them try to come up with more numbers. They can do it laying on the floor if it's easier. Also, have two or more kids work together to create numbers. *Activity teaches functional freedom as they see that even their bodies can represent other things such as numbers and helps reinforce math concepts as children take a close look at the shape of individual numbers, processing this in a physical way and therefore giving them a more concrete view of numbers.*

TELL ME, HORSIE, HOW MANY?

Have the children pretend they are horses, getting down on their hands and knees, whinnying and prancing around. Ask the "horsies" simple math questions and have them stomp out the answers! For one plus one, they stomp two times. *Children love to pretend to be animals, and this stimulus freedom activity allows them to be horses but combine it with some learning fun.*

RAINBOW IN THE SKY

You will need an overhead projector or a large flashlight for this. Put the projector on the floor and flip the top back so the light is shining directly up at the ceiling. Have the children lay on the floor, looking up at the ceiling. Place a color paddle on the overhead. (Color paddles are made of transparent plastic and are available in assorted colors from most school-supply catalogs.) Ask the children what color they see. Put up the three primary colors one at a time and discuss them, asking the children about things they know that are those colors. Next, layer two of the color paddles to create a new color. Leave a corner of each paddle exposed so they can see each original color, plus the new one in the middle. As you use the paddles to create new colors, talk with the children about how colors combine. After you've shown them the colors, allow them to sit up and use the paddles themselves to see what colors they can create on their own. *Activity supports stimulus freedom as a lesson is taught with children laying on their backs rather than sitting as it also teaches color combining.*

LEAF MATCHING

During the fall, when there is an abundance of brightly colored leaves, take a leaf walk and collect them in different shapes, sizes, and colors. Find two leaves of each variety that match as closely as possible. Next, either laminate the leaves with a laminating machine, or cover them on both sides using clear contact paper. Cut them out, leaving a half-inch border to keep the leaf inside intact. Give these to the children to match up. They can also be sorted by leaf variety or color or size. *Activity supports stimulus freedom as children use nature to learn math.*

JAR GUESSING

Collect a variety of lidded jars in different shapes and sizes. Fill the jars with small items (one type in each jar) such as marbles, pennies, thumbtacks, beads, and so on. Have each child guess how many of the items are in each jar. Dump the items out and count them together, lining them up in groups of 10 for easier counting of large numbers. Children work with estimating and graphing as well as practice counting. *Activity supports stimulus freedom as children see items in jars as something to count and consider the possibility for counting other objects they find in jars (such as pickles or cherries).*

SCIENCE

VEGGIE DYES

Take a walk outdoors and have the children collect different types of vegetation: flowers, grasses, leaves, berries, and so on. Set out several large cups or small bowls filled with water. Place the vegetation in the cups, one type per cup. Allow them to sit for up to a week, adding water if needed to keep the containers filled, and taking note each day of how the water changes. At the end of the week, place a piece of white cotton material in each cup (a white tee shirt cut into squares, or handkerchiefs, will work nicely). Allow the material to sit in the water overnight. The next day, check to see which cloths were dyed and which were not. Talk about the difference between the color of the item in the water and the color it dyed the fabric. Talk about why those that did not produce a dye didn't and why those that did were successful. *Activity spans over a week and therefore supports delayed gratification as well as allowing time for children to use their imaginations to consider the possible outcomes while exploring science concepts of color and fabric content.*

BERRY PAINTS

If possible, take a walk in a meadow or woods that has berries growing, such as on a mulberry tree or raspberry or blackberry bushes. Collect berries in small plastic buckets. If you don't have an area like this to visit, buy a variety of berries from the grocery store—raspberries, blackberries, and blueberries work best. Help the children to create their own paints from the berries. Put a handful of berries in a cup and crush them using a spoon. Add a teaspoon or so of flour to thicken it up a bit and mix well. You don't have to thicken it—leaving it thin will have it work like watercolors; thicker will be closer to tempera paints. Give the children white paper to paint on. Different berries will create different colors. Allow the children free expression with what they paint. *Activity supports stimulus freedom as berries are used in a new way, and painting without rules always allows for creativity to thrive while giving children a creative outlet as they express themselves through painting.*

FLOWER POWER

Explore with the children the many uses of a flower. Collect some brightly colored flowers such as pansies, roses, lilies, violets, or impatiens. Let the children's imaginations really go to work as they think of many uses for the flowers. Provide examples and nudges to get them started, but allow them to take it wherever it leads them, such as "We can cook with them. So what happens when we boil them, or bake them, or fry them? What is the product we get and what can we do with it?" (Example: If you boil rose petals, you will have scented rose water to use as a perfume, and the petals can be pressed and rolled into balls, stuck on needles to dry, and will make sweet-smelling beads for necklaces.) Flowers can also be pressed or pounded. Experiment with pressing them between sheets of paper or other items and pounding them with various items on different types of paper (put the flower between two sheets of heavy paper and hit with a mallet or hammer). Different flowers will provide different results. Flowers can be dried by hanging them upside down in bunches, and then used to make potpourri or dried-flower arrangements. As the children come up with different ideas and experiments, provide the tools and supplies they need to fully explore an outcome. *Activity supports stimulus freedom as flowers are seen as something other than just flowers, and creative expression as art is explored through many different mediums.*

TOUCH TRAYS

Provide a table for exploration of similar items with some differences, such as different types of leaves, grasses, dirt, or other items from nature. Allow the children time to explore each item closely. Provide magnifying glasses if possible. Have them discuss the differences and similarities they see in each set. *Activity supports balanced-brain thinking as they use their senses of sight, touch, and smell to explore the items, and then compare what they've found to come to conclusions regarding similarities and differences.*

SCARF TERRAIN

Use a collection of scarves of different sizes, colors, patterns, and materials. Support the children's sense of functional freedom by giving the scarves to the children and asking them to find scarves to represent different types of terrain—sand, water, dirt, pavement, mountains, woods, grass, and so on. Then have them lay the scarves out on the floor to build a "terrain" land-scape. Provide them toy cars, boats, and other vehicles to play with on this new terrain. *Activity supports functional freedom as scarves are seen as terrain rather than material while helping children explore their world and the many types of surfaces in it.*

Activity extender: Do the same activities, only instead of using toy vehicles, let the children walk through the new terrain without wearing shoes. As they walk on the scarves, discuss how different each feels on their feet, or ask them to act out what they would do differently to travel through this terrain by swimming, climbing, hopping, running, and so on. *As children act out these different modes of travel, the activity then meets standards for physical activity while still supporting functional freedom and science.*

PLANTING TIME

Plant a variety of seeds in different cups or pots on the same day. Have the children guess which will grow first, tallest, with the most leaves, and so on. Then track the plants' growth on a daily basis to find the answers. *The activity combines the use of delayed gratification with a growing knowledge of differences in plants and how they grow.*

ANIMAL SOUNDS

Make tapes of animal sounds from the same species but different breeds. For example, a tape of cat sounds that includes a housecat, a lion, a tiger, and a bobcat. Visit a zoo to get the sounds or look for them on the Internet. Do the same for dogs: Barks from different-sized dogs will sound very different. A pet store is a good place to start collecting the sounds, which can become an activity in itself. Once you have them, allow the children to listen to the tape, try to imitate the sounds, match them to a photo of the animal, and discuss the differences. *Activity supports balanced-brain thinking as children use their sense of hearing to identify sounds and begin to classify what they have heard and analyze it.*

DON'T EAT THE BREAD!

Give each child a slice of bread (any kind works) and a resealable plastic sandwich bag. Have them write their names on their bags using permanent markers and then place their pieces of bread inside, closing the bags tightly. Place the bread bags inside a drawer or dark cupboard. Have the children estimate how many days they think it will be before they see mold growing on their bread. Create a chart for each child to mark the process. Each day, check the bread and note whether or not any mold is found. Once they see mold appear, discuss how they did with their estimates. Then have them estimate when the slices will be completely covered with mold. Continue checking the bread each day and charting and discussing its progress. Once a slice is completely covered, check the estimate and discuss the process. You may want to give different types of bread to different children so they can also compare how different kinds performed. Homemade bread will grow mold the fastest as it has no preservatives. Store-bought bread will go different lengths depending on the preservatives. Some may even take weeks to grow mold! To prevent the children from coming in direct contact with the mold at any time, do not open the bags once they are sealed. When the activity is done, throw the bread and bags away. *Activity supports delayed gratification as children watch and wait during the process and explores the science behind mold growth.*

UP, UP, AND AWAY

Purchase a helium balloon, the larger the better. Have the children collect items from the room to see if the balloon will lift them up. Be sure there is a range from very small to very heavy or large. Have the children arrange the items from smallest to largest. Beginning with the largest, have each child guess whether or not the balloon will be able to lift it. Tie the balloon to the item and let go. Continue down the line with each item, guessing first, then tying and letting go each time until you come to an item that the balloon lifts. Hopefully, if you have a good variety of items, there will be some that come up only a few inches or less, and as lighter items are used they will rise higher, ending with an item that allows the balloon to rise all the way up to the ceiling! *Activity supports functional freedom along with the rules of science as items are explored and used as weights rather than as the items they are. It also supports delayed gratification as the children wait and anticipate which item will finally allow the balloon to rise.*

SOUND SCAVENGER HUNT

Begin the activity using concrete sounds, asking the children to find the things in the room that produce that sound. Examples are ticking (clock), dripping (faucet), clicking (shoes on hard floor), a bang (door slam), a ring (phone or bell). Next, expand on the simple science of sounds we know to challenge the children into abstract thinking by asking them to find something in the room that has the sound of happiness, freedom, laziness, quickness, or fear. Name emotions and see how the children relate those emotions to concrete objects. *Activity supports sound recognition (science development) while expanding on children's ability to use both sides of the brain and connect the concrete with the abstract.*

WIGGLY WORMS

Give the children sleeping bags to crawl into, asking them to get in all the way and hold the open end tight around their chests with their hands and arms inside. Tell the children they are now going to be worms and to begin to move about the room as a worm would. As the children move, have them discuss what is fun about moving this way, and what is hard. Provide a large pile of pillows for the children to "dig" into as a worm would dig into dirt. Is it easier to dig up or down? What would a worm do? Do they think a worm moves slowly or fast? Help the children to see that by looking at items (such as a sleeping bag) in a new way, they will discover more props for their dramatic play situations. Ask them what other item they could use to pretend to be a worm. A pillow case? A blanket they roll up in? *Activity explores the movement of worms as well as functional freedom as they consider the variety of possible props.*

SOCIAL AND EMOTIONAL DEVELOPMENT

BONDS OF FRIENDSHIP

Provide the children with a basketful of long pieces of rope or balls of yarn. Tell the children they can use them to wrap around toys, each other, trees—anything they like—to create a large web. Once they are done, tell them they will now need to work together to wind the rope or yarn back up. One child starts, and as others are unwrapped, they join in to help untangle the rope. Children will need to work together to keep the rope from becoming even more tangled. Adults can help if a knot appears too tough for the children to get apart. *Activity supports creativity as they build the web and curiosity as they work to solve the problem of unraveling it. Activity also supports physical development—both large and small motor—as they move to unravel the rope.*

NONPUPPET PUPPET SHOW

Give the children an array of items to put on a puppet show—a paintbrush, an oven mitt, a glove, a skillet, and so on—but no puppets! Have them animate the items and create a play based on them. *Activity supports functional freedom as items are given "life" through their dialog and children explore a variety of social interaction situations through the puppetry.*

COOPERATIVE MUSICAL GAMES

Play classic games such as farmer in the dell, ring-around-the-rosy, and musical chairs. To get the most out of these activities, allow children to choose among themselves the roles they will play. Encourage them to share their thoughts and feelings during and after the game has been played. Take turns so they all get a chance to play the roles they would like. For musical chairs, instead of removing a chair each turn, have the child without a chair sit on the lap of another child. As the game progresses, you will end up with one long line of children sitting on another's lap! Finding ways to alter games so that everyone can participate and feel rewarded, rather than left out or punished, should be the goal for all cooperative games. When choosing music, take the opportunity to use a variety of musical genres, and have the children or teacher or parent sing. *These games use balanced-brain activities through music, sequencing, and decision making and combine it with the physical activity of the movement to the music and social development as the children learn to play cooperatively.*

I'M FEELING A BIT MUSICAL

Help children express feelings through music and movement. Processing music into a physical activity is a strong balanced-brain activity—and lots of fun! Play a variety of music—different genres, tempos, and volumes—and ask the children how the music makes them *feel*. Have them put a name to these feelings and then act them out through dance and movement to the music. Between songs, ask the children what situations would make them feel the way the song did. *This supports balanced-brain activity by combining the musical with the physical while teaching children how to use music as a form of creative expression of their feelings.*

WE'RE IN THIS TOGETHER!

Children who are shy will feel more at ease working with a group on a song or dance. Allow these children chances to express themselves without feeling shy by providing lots of opportunities for group dancing. Avoid having one child stand out, such as asking someone to come to the middle of the circle to dance. Children who are shy will feel more at ease with the activity if they know it doesn't involve any pressure to stand out from the crowd. Yet by encouraging them to do their own interpretations of dance and movement during the song (rather than instructing children to all follow an adult's lead), you are easing shy children into a sense of independence. As they participate more in these types of activities, they will build the confidence to step away from the crowd to showcase their abilities. *Activity supports stimulus freedom as children feel able to create their individual dances rather than following the dance steps of others and helps engage them in creative expression through dance.*

SILLY FACE, SILLY FACE, WHAT DO YOU SEE?

Have the children choose from a selection of faces, either drawings or photos, of different emotions such as happy, sad, sleepy, mad, and surprised. They can be mounted on circles of paper with sticks attached to make puppets. Create a silly face for you to begin with. Sit in a circle and have the children hold up their face puppets. Begin by saying to your face puppet, "Silly Face, Silly Face, what do you see?" Then hold up the puppet, have it look to the puppet face held by the child on your right, and say in a silly voice, "I see a [name the emotion for the face you see] face looking at me!" Then, continuing in the silly voice, say to the child, "_____ face, _____ face, what do you see?" Now that child uses a voice to match the face he or she is holding, has the puppet look to the next child's face puppet, and answers, "I see a _____ face looking at me!" The child continues with, "_____ face, _____ face, what do you see?" And the next child answers. This continues around the circle until it returns to the teacher, each child answering with what that child sees and then asking the next child what that child sees. *Activity supports creativity through stimulus freedom as children openly name emotions of others and meets standards for social development as children learn to recognize emotion through facial expressions.*

FAMILY WORK DAY

This can be done any time of year but fits well in spring. Hold a Family Work Day, where families are invited on a weekend day to help clear the playground or yard. Or build something new together for the children such as a new play structure, fort, garden, or sandbox. Provide the necessary tools and materials and make a potluck out of it, providing a main dish and utensils while each family also provides a dish to pass. Involve the children as much as possible, letting them rake leaves or dead grass, do a bucket brigade with the sand from a trailer to the sandbox, and so on. Take advantage of any talents the families have, such as construction or gardening knowledge. The day will provide lots of opportunity for the adults to model cooperative behavior for the children. *The activity supports creativity through stimulus freedom as it will be unusual to come to the school or day care on a weekend and spend the day there with their parents, working on something together.*

FROSTY THE SNOWMAN

Next time you get a fresh snowfall of sticky snow, head outside to build Frosty! Spend time together packing snow into small balls and rolling them until they are large. Children can work together to push the larger, heavy balls. Once three balls are assembled into a snowman, encourage the children to think of things they can use to create a face, arms, or clothing for the snowman. Allow the suggestions to include items both outside in nature and inside, such as sticks, rocks, and leaves, or raisins, carrots, and toy dishes. Provide old clothing such as hats, gloves, or scarves. You can build several snowmen and use different types of items to create the faces on each. Just remember when you're done to join hands in a circle around your snowman and sing the traditional song—"Frosty the Snowman!" *Activity supports creativity through the functional freedom of using objects to create faces, arms, and clothing as well as supports social skills through cooperative building of the snowman.*

FAMILY PHOTO MIX-UP

Ask the families to provide photos of each family member, preferably a full body shot. Copy the photos (don't cut the originals!), increasing their size so each person is approximately one foot tall. Give the children a large sheet of construction paper and tell them they will get to create a new family member! Allow them to cut features from each of the family's photos to mix together and glue onto the paper, creating a new person. They can use Mom's eyes, Dad's ears, Grandma's face, Grandpa's body, baby brother's nose, and their own hair. *Activity supports creativity through stimulus freedom as the features of family members are mixed up and meets social learning standards as children spend time closely observing their own family members and comparing their differences and similarities.*

COGNITIVE DEVELOPMENT

See previous chapter.

HEALTH AND PHYSICAL DEVELOPMENT

UPSIDE-DOWN PUZZLES

To support stimulus freedom, present children with a jigsaw puzzle but place the pieces upside down. Encourage the children to focus on the shapes of the pieces in order to fit them together and finish the puzzle. *Activity supports hand/eye coordination and small motor development as well as creativity through stimulus freedom.*

TASTING PARTIES

Provide the children with food samples. Go beyond discussing taste and have children describe other things the food may make them think of—a movie, a song, a feeling, a color. *Activity supports stimulus freedom as they make connections between food and other things as well as provides opportunity for exploration of new, healthy foods.*

NAME WRITING

Have the children practice writing their names in creative mediums rather than just pencil or crayon. Give them a shallow tray with sand, salt, or sugar in it and have them use their fingers or small sticks to write their names. Do the same outside in the sandbox using a large stick. Spray shaving cream on the table. After playing with it awhile, it will reduce to a thin film of white on the table. Then children can use their fingers to draw their names in it. On a dry patch of dirt, have the children use a small watering can to "draw" their names in the dirt with water. *Activity supports functional freedom as children see items as possible writing instruments while giving them more physical ways to explore literacy.*

BASEBALL MUSICIANS

Hang a variety of items from a clothesline outside in a roomy area. The items should include things that would make a sound when hit by a ball and some that would not make a sound, such as a pillowcase. Give children a ball to throw, having them stand back 10 feet or more from the targets. Ask them to throw the ball at the items that will make a sound. *This activity combines gross motor skills with originality, expanding the children's view of what can make noise and how it can be made.*

SURPRISE PUZZLES

Using a computer or copy machine, make a large copy of a photograph the kids will enjoy, such as animals or their class photo. Glue it onto a piece of lightweight cardboard, putting a thin layer of glue over the entire photo for protection. When dry, cut the photo into puzzle pieces. Give the puzzle to the children when they can't see it together and do not tell them what the picture is. Have the children complete the puzzle. *Activity supports small motor development through use of puzzle pieces while teaching children to move forward when faced with ambiguity. Encouraging them to take a risk by doing an unknown puzzle supports their sense of creativity—they will be better equipped to face new challenges.*

ROLLING HILLS

Encourage children to roll down large hills. They can choose how to roll—on their sides, head over heels, fast or slow. Don't forget to join in the fun! *Activity combines large motor skills with teaching children to take risks and discover something new through their actions.*

TIME TO MOVE

Engage the children in helping clear out a room for a day. Have them pick up toys, move book shelves and furniture to the sides, roll up carpets, and so on. After all of the heavy work is done and all the items have been put up against the walls or otherwise out of the way, you now have a big open space for some large motor activity such as tag, leap frog, or dancing! When the activities are done, have the children help move everything back. *Activity supports stimulus freedom as children see a new way to enjoy a space previously used for something else while giving them the space they need to do more large motor activities inside.*

MILK CARTON TOWERS

Collect a large bin of empty milk cartons, both small and large. (Be sure to clean them out well with soap and water, and let dry.) Close some tops in their normal position with duct tape. Flatten the tops of others and tape down. Take them outside for the children to play with and build towers. They are lightweight, so the towers will tumble easily (which kids love), but aside from building towers, they can line them up and see how far across the lawn they will go, use them to create outlines (like a blueprint) of walls to play house in, or create other designs on the lawn (like a smiley face!). *Activity supports functional freedom as they consider new items for building supplies while giving them a physical activity with ranges depending on the size of the boxes.*

GET CREATIVE WITH PLAY-DOH

Next time you get out the Play-Doh or clay for the children, don't include any items related to food, such as cookie cutters, rolling pins, silverware, or cups. Instead, give them something to stretch their imaginations a little further such as feathers, pipe cleaners, pinecones, rocks, toy cars, wooden blocks, necklaces, paper clips, rubber bands, sticks, and leaves. See how it makes a difference in how they view the clay and its possibilities. *Activity supports stimulus freedom since cooking items typically dictate to the children to create food items, but a variety of odd items will allow the children the freedom to think of many other items to create as they use small motor skills to make their creations.*

THE ARTS

WHAT'S YOUR CREATIVE EXPRESSION?

Invite artists to speak to your class. Include painters, sculptors, textile artists, jewelry designers, glassblowers, photographers, and so on. Ask them to share with the children how they feel they are able to express themselves and their creativity through their mediums. If possible, invite several at the same time, or on sequential days, to foster discussion about the differences in each form of art expression. Ask your visitors to share with the children how they are inspired to create their art and in what ways they look differently at everyday things and experiences in our society. For example, a painter may look at trees and see them not as trees, but as filters for light, and notice how the light affects the colors of each of the leaves. A sculptor may see the "junk" in your trashcan as items of shape and color that can be combined to create something new. A photographer may describe seeing the world through a frame and how each element complements the other in that frame. A jeweler may select colors of beads based on feelings. Help the children ask questions, preparing before the visit by discussing what types of questions they might ask. After the visit, encourage children to be inspired by what they learned and use art supplies to express their own creativity in the ways described by the guests. *Activity supports balanced-brain activity as children use all of their senses to learn about art expression as they look at the artist's work and listen to how it was created, and then use their own sense of touch and sight to create their own work. Activity also supports functional freedom as artists explain the many ways they look at the world to create their works of art. Activity also supports curiosity and courtesy through the question-and-answer discussion and the respect shown to each speaker.*

Activity extender: Consider inviting guest speakers who use other forms of creative expression, such as writers, singers, actors, dancers, and so on. Follow the same ideas in creating questions beforehand and allowing children to mimic the forms they identified with or were inspired by.

MUSICAL ART

Provide children with large sheets of paper to paint on, preferably on easels. Give them several colors of paint. Then play a variety of music for the children. Ask the children to close their eyes and feel the music, then to open their eyes and use the paints to paint the music and how they feel. Encourage the children to use their bodies—to sway their arms to the music while brushing on the paint—and to use colors they feel best represent the music. After the song has ended, choose another song with a completely different tempo and tone. Again, have the children first close their eyes to feel the music, then to paint in response to the music. You may have the children either paint on new paper or simply continue over their first painting. When the song is finished, have the children discuss how they painted differently for the two songs. You may continue this with as many songs as you wish. Focus on the stimulus freedom of inspiration coming not from a visual but an auditory source. The paintings should reflect movement, not specific objects; the process holds importance, not the painted result. Use the results only as a way to compare the types of music and how they were represented. *Activity supports stimulus freedom as children connect sounds to artistic expressions while getting to create a reflection of their own feelings induced by the sound through art. Activity also supports curiosity through the questions and answers and through discovery of the results of the painting session.*

PAINTING THE HOUSE

Provide the children with a large plastic cup or small bucket filled with shaving cream and large paintbrushes. Have children "paint" a playhouse, swing set, picnic table, or other large outside structure until it is completely covered. The item can be easily hosed off when finished to clean up. *Children love this opportunity for stimulus freedom. Painting on a toy is typically not allowed; bending this rule supports their creativity and also supports their artistic skill building in using a large brush.*

MUD POTS

After a good rain, have children go with you to collect mud in a bucket and bring inside. If you don't have an area where mud can be collected, make your own with store-bought dirt mixed with water. Make the mixture the consistency of soft clay. Give each child about one cup of mud on a newspaper-covered table. Have them form the mud, as they would clay, into a bowl. Encourage them to embellish the bowl with small bits of mud. Let the bowls dry outside in the sun, and then have the children paint them. *This activity integrates stimulus freedom (playing with mud is typically against the rules) with functional freedom (using something other than clay to make a bowl) along with typical art expression through pottery.*

TREASURE BOX

Collect odd items in a large box with a lid to be labeled "Treasure Box." Banker boxes work well. Collect typical collage items (buttons, yarn, paper, sequins, felt, and so on) and nontraditional items (spice containers, cereal boxes, wooden spools, pieces of chain, Frisbees, a pair of jeans). Present children with the box and provide materials for them to put together the items inside, such as glue, tape, string, elastic, and rubber bands. Give children complete freedom to create what they want from the materials. Creations can be 3-D (such as sculptures or buildings) or 2-D (such as paintings or drawings), with or without moving parts. *Activity allows for both functional and stimulus freedom and supports artist expression.*

SUN BLOCK DESIGNS

Provide children with a variety of wooden blocks of different sizes and shapes and a piece of dark-colored construction paper—purples and blues work well. In the early morning, go outside and on a flat surface that is in the sun all day, have the children place their sheets of paper down, and then arrange the blocks into a design on the paper. Leave the blocks and paper alone and at noon come out and take off about half the blocks. At the end of the day, remove the rest of the blocks and look at the designs. The sun will fade the paper, and because it is moving, it will create shapes that do not have sharp edges in the areas where blocks were left all day. *Activity supports delayed gratification and shows children how things change with time as well as teaches alternative approaches to creating art.*

WILLABY WALLABY WOO

This song is great for creative expression, showing children how to be silly yet also giving them practice with rhyming (literacy) and rhythm.

To do the song, sing the original first, then change the underlined words: In the first line, change it to a name of a child; in the second line, change it to any silly word that rhymes with the name of the child; and on the third line, use the *W* as the first letter, then add the ending of the child's name. On the fourth line, use the child's name again.

Willaby Wallaby *Woo*

An elephant stepped on *you!*

Willaby Wallaby *Wee*

An elephant stepped on *me!*

Willaby Wallaby *Pat*

An elephant stepped on *Zat!*

Willaby Wallaby *Wat*

An elephant stepped on *Pat!*

Activity supports stimulus freedom as children change lyrics while practicing rhyme and rhythm.

DIVA DESIGNERS

Take your dress-up box to a new level. In addition to traditional clothing items, add nontraditional items and model for the children to get them started on the possibilities. Examples are a pot or pillowcase as a hat, a rubber hose as a belt, a rug as a cape, a tablecloth as a dress, a garland of flowers as a necklace, and so on. Ask the children for ideas and be ready to provide the props. *Activity integrates dramatic play with functional freedom.*

NAME THAT TUNE

Play a familiar tune for the children. Then help them to make up their own words to the song. You can start out simple, such as substituting just a word or two—for example, "Mary had a little lamb" can become "Adam had a little dog." Then, as they get the idea, encourage them to make up more of the song. To help them construct lyrics to match the song, on a chalkboard or large sheet of paper, draw underlines to indicate the number of syllables needed for a line of the song. For example, the beginning of "Mary Had a Little Lamb" would be "Ma·ry had a lit·tle lamb, lit·tle lamb, lit·tle lamb, Ma·ry had a lit·tle lamb his fleece was white as snow." This is 26 syllables. And we know that the first seven will be repeated. This also helps teach children the correlation of lyrics to notes in a song. Each syllable will be another note in the song. For those of you with music experience, you can draw the notes above the word blanks as well. So the children need a sentence with seven syllables. This may be a hard concept for them, but you can guide them by using a drum or rhythm stick to show how each syllable goes with a beat in the music. Their sentence could be "Tom Z. likes to run outside." (See how it's the syllables, not the words, that matter in matching it to the tune?) Children actually do this very easily on their own many times. They can take a tune and substitute words without ever really understanding or seeing the structure, but it's a good extender on the activity to show them how the rhythm and notes affect the words. *Activity supports stimulus freedom as children see songs as something to change and build off of rather than as a stand alone activity while teaching children rhythm and musical notes.*

Teaching Curiosity 4

Creativity and curiosity are intrinsically linked. One leads to the other and vice versa. They are both important elements of problem solving. We begin by trying something new (creativity) and then test it to see what happens (curiosity). But the opposite can also occur, where we begin by looking to discover all the possibilities (curiosity) and then use this information in a new way (creativity) to solve our problem. This give-and-take between the two can lead to many exciting and new revelations and possibilities. They are the keys for many an inventor, engineer, or philosopher in making new inventions, solutions, and discoveries. Children who are given the freedom to stretch these abilities and explore their capabilities within them to the fullest will find their play to have a richer, deeper meaning and a higher sense of accomplishment. Ginger Carlson (2008), author of *Child of Wonder*, ties together curiosity and learning: "Exploration is the foundation for developing a creative thinker" (p. 18).

Given the importance of curiosity to the evolution of our society through new inventions and ideas, one would think it would hold a higher importance in our educational system. Unfortunately, we have moved to such results-oriented educational experiences that instead of being provided an open field of exploration, our children are being led down specific paths, both figuratively and literally.

All too often, curriculums are filled with experiences that lead to specific results rather than an open end. In an attempt to meet state early learning standards, activities are designed to lead children step-by-step through specific learning goals. Even the science experiments are meant to lead children to a predisposed conclusion, leaving curiosity far behind.

Children are learning to follow directions, to make the connections that have been laid out for them, but to think no further than that. There are even times when children are chastised for stepping outside of the boundaries to question the activity or result. An agenda has been set, and for many teachers, time is of the essence in teaching specific results. In my own daughter's middle school, the parents were told that the previously taught English class was being completely changed in order to teach only what would be offered on the state tests our children were expected to complete at the end of the year. The result was that free exploration of many topics was completely eliminated from the curriculum.

I learned the long-term effects of this type of curriculum from a parent who had a son in my preschool. He and his wife were professors in science at the University of Wisconsin in Madison. He said that my program's focus on the three *C*s is what drew them to my preschool. He told me how he felt that curiosity and creativity were lacking in many of the young adults he sees in his classes and of his concern about this. He explained how, when given a problem, his students seem capable only of reciting previously learned solutions. They are often unable to follow their natural curiosities in order to learn; they follow only in the direction he leads them. This also prevents them from being creative in their problem solving—it doesn't occur to them to push their learning, to look elsewhere for answers, or to imagine new solutions. He agreed that by supporting curiosity in his young son's play, we would be laying a foundation for much further learning as he grew older.

As the grade schools deal with the problem of creating curriculum to produce specific test results, and the colleges face the unintended consequences, it becomes increasingly necessary for early childhood educators and parents to avoid these pitfalls and work to establish a solid base of curiosity in children that can sustain their learning for years to come. In early childhood, we feel these pressures to move into results-based learning. But lucky for us, hidden deep under "cognitive development" in many of our state standards lay the opportunities to foster curiosity in children. Standards such as "notices new things and people," "investigates

Ethan Solves a Problem

I was sitting on the couch in my day care, surrounded by children, reading them a book. Jack was on my lap, and several of the other children were trying their personal techniques for obtaining that coveted spot. Alexis was slowly moving in, wiggling a toe under Jack and trying to be smooth. Hannah tried a more direct approach, standing in front of me, her back to me, and moving backward until she bumped into Jack and continued to bump him, hoping he'd move. Throughout this, Ethan was sitting quietly to my right, even moving away from me to the end of the couch. After a few minutes, Ethan got up and began to walk around the room. Soon he had the toy vacuum and nonchalantly began pushing it around the room, eventually ending up near the couch. Then he sat back on the end of the couch with a very satisfied smile.

What Ethan knew from hours of curious observation was that Jack loved that vacuum more than anything, including sitting on my lap. Ethan's plan worked perfectly, as within seconds Jack spotted the vacuum and hopped off my lap just as Ethan slid in and claimed the front-row view!

items closely," or "asks questions and provides answers" give us that window of opportunity to include curiosity activities into our programs. For those states that have not included such openings, it is still possible to bring curiosity back into our classrooms and back into childhood.

Joan Beck (1999), who in the 1990s pioneered coverage of new research on brain development and is the author of *How to Raise a Brighter Child*, reports that "a child has a built-in drive to explore, to investigate, to seek excitement and novelty, to learn by using every one of his senses, to satisfy his boundless curiosity. And this drive is just as innate as hunger, thirst, the avoidance of pain, and other drives previously identified by psychologists as primary" (p. 51). She warns us that because curiosity has not been recognized as a basic drive, that many actions of children become misinterpreted. Children who are simply following their natural curious instincts are often labeled as naughty or misbehaving. "Bright youngsters with an abundance of curiosity are often considered troublemakers in schools that fail to understand their great need for learning stimulation" (p. 51).

I've often had children in my preschool over the years who seem to "get into everything." Most teachers at one time or another do. While many other adults see this as troublesome, I and teachers like me see this as a challenge to provide these children with what they need by creating more interesting projects and activities, providing a larger variety of choices, and tapping into this natural curiosity to see how it might just take the entire group on an

adventure toward learning. These children were very content when presented with many choices and options to explore; they also became wonderful role models for others during times of exploration, asking the questions others didn't think of, searching for answers in creative ways. Rather than viewing these children as naughty, teachers and parents can actually benefit from the enthusiasm they bring to their work and the diversity in their journeys toward answers.

Before diagnosis, many children with attention-deficit/hyperactivity disorder (ADHD) are seen as those who get into everything. Even after diagnosis, many teachers view this behavior as troublesome, and much

Famous People With ADHD

Bill Cosby	"Magic" Johnson
Cher	Michael Jordan
Jim Carey	Leonardo da Vinci
Robin Williams	Thomas Edison
Will Smith	Benjamin Franklin
Whoopi Goldberg	Alexander Graham Bell
Danny Glover	Sir Isaac Newton
Pablo Picasso	Albert Einstein
Vincent van Gogh	Prince Charles
Ansel Adams	John F. Kennedy
Bruce Jenner	Walt Disney
Nolan Ryan	Henry Ford
Pete Rose	Malcolm Forbes
Babe Ruth	

is done to control it. However, I think it is very interesting for teachers and parents—and even these children—to know that many very famous people had ADHD. This list includes Pablo Picasso, Albert Einstein, Abraham Lincoln, and many more. (See sidebar on page 63.) These people were all celebrated for their immense abilities to think outside the box and explore the possibilities—which is all they were doing when they were getting into everything!

One of the basics of supporting a sense of exploration in children is encouraging them in knowing they have the power to learn—the ability to follow their passions and find answers. A simple way my own family instilled this attitude of further exploration is by banning the word *can't*. Whenever one of us four girls came to my parents with a sentence that began with "I can't," we were quickly corrected with "It's not that you can't; it's that you haven't found a way to do it *yet*." That was our cue to explore new ways until we could figure it out.

As with creativity, modeling curiosity is an important element in bringing it back into our children's lives. In *More Help! For Teachers of Young Children*, author Gwen Snyder (2006) writes, "We live in a wonderfully fascinating world, and if we present it with a joyful spirit of exploration, we can help children keep their natural curiosity" (p. 8). She shares just how simple this can be by saying to our children, "Wow, this is exciting. I want to know more." She calls this curiosity "food for the brain." Children naturally feed off their curiosity to learn new things and accomplish new feats.

We can support our children's natural ability to be curious, and to link this curiosity into creativity and problem solving, by supporting the following factors:

- **Explore the possibilities**: Wonder, experiment, tell stories
- **Explore the world**: Field trips and dress-up
- **Ask questions**: The five *W*s and how

When we bring these factors into our classrooms and homes, we give our children the opportunities to cultivate their natural sense of curiosity, to build on their creativity, and to become problem solvers.

EXPLORE THE POSSIBILITIES

Teachers and parents can foster an environment for children that encourages their questions and sense of exploration simply by staying completely open to possibilities in the children's questions and abilities. By doing so, teachers and parents will keep the doors open for the children in their care.

Allowing ourselves and our children to be curious is as simple as letting them work to finish the sentence "I wonder . . ." In *The Art of the Possible*, Dawna Markova (1991) tells us: "Rather than merely accumulating new theories and more information that will be outmoded in a few years, our focus must shift to learning *how* to learn" (pp. 2–3). She encourages us to "just allow your unconscious mind to kaleidoscope, your curiosity to pulse on: 'I wonder . . . I wonder how or when I . . .'" (p. 172). She refers to this as being "old fashioned curious." And it does seem like an old-fashioned idea to many. We've spent years accumulating information and working to teach this information to children. What we've forgotten is that this information was discovered in the first place because someone got curious.

Scientists take curiosity very seriously. It is the essence of what they do. They have a curiosity about a particular thing or idea, and they begin to explore. They wonder. They ask all those questions: "Why?" "What if . . . ?" "I wonder . . ." One of the hallmarks of curiosity in science is that it is more than just wondering—scientists actually follow through. They test; they make multiple attempts to make something work or fail. They build upon their first question and continue to experiment. When the "I wonder if it could . . ." doesn't work out, they immediately jump to "Why didn't it?" And when they find this answer, it leads them to yet another question to explore: "So now what?" It's a never-ending quest for information. Sound a lot like some of your three-year-olds?

Young children are born scientists. They want all the information they can get, and they are willing to work to find it. And when their questions are answered, they will come up with new questions. When they are told they have acquired the information and the quest has ended, the excitement for this exploration begins to fade. Children who are presented with information that does not lead to further learning stop chasing after the deeper meaning and simply accept that there is no more. This leads to a generation of children who do not question, who do not delve into a deep understanding of concepts, but instead simply learn what the concepts are and accept that they exist.

This is why teaching curiosity—supporting the quest and desire to

How to Eat a Peanut Butter and Jelly Sandwich

By Mikey (age 3)

First take the two pieces of bread apart.

Use fingers to lick up the jelly.

Pull the crust off the jelly part.

Eat the jelly bread.

Eat the pulled-off crust.

Use fingers to lick up the peanut butter.

Take the crust off the peanut butter part.

Eat the peanut butter bread.

Eat the crusts.

Ask for more!

explore—is so important for our children's further learning and development. When children have curiosity, they look beyond the whole to notice the parts; they pay attention to details and the interaction of them. By observation, they learn how the interaction of different parts affects the outcome. When the interactions of the parts change, the outcome changes. Children who understand that by exploring the details they may discover not only the answer to the concept but how this concept is conceived, how its parts interact, how it interacts with the world, and how all of these components can be manipulated are our future scientists. Without this quest, we cannot cure cancer, create earth-friendly fuel, save our rainforests, or end hunger. All of these accomplishments will involve doing so much more than learning the facts.

It's about trying the impossible. Scientists face every day what most people think may be impossible—and they find a way to make it possible. They brainstorm the different ways they know of to try something, and when none of them work, they take what they learned through the process to come up with even more ways to try. Sometimes, they even find more than one way!

Support children's scientists within by presenting them with situations where they can try the impossible, experiment, learn from mistakes, and celebrate the multiple answers. Rejoice in the possibilities children see in every situation. Let their creativity merge with their curiosity to take them to new and exciting places.

Children are also natural dreamers. They can lay on their back in the grass, gazing up at the clear blue sky and dream of living in a castle made of ice cream, riding on a dinosaur, growing 20 feet tall. This dreaming is the perfect merging of creativity and curiosity. They begin by wondering, and in their dreams they make it happen.

For this reason, stories are a wonderful way to support a child's curiosity. In a story, things are explored, created, imagined. In nonfiction, children's curiosity is fed with information that they need about the world. In fiction, they explore the possibilities of the world around them.

Daniel Pink (2006) identifies six "senses" that he attributes to higher intelligence. One of these is "story." By learning stories, rather than straight facts, we are better able to remember things. What this means for parents and teachers is that when teaching our children, we should present facts by sharing the story behind the facts. The famous children's book author Eric Carle uses this technique to bring the insect and animal world alive for children. He shares with children an insect's or animal's story, and through the story the children learn many facts. In *The Very Hungry Caterpillar* (Carle, 1969), a caterpillar eats and eats, piquing a child's curiosity about why a caterpillar would want to eat so much. Then, in the end, the child discovers that it is part of the process for the caterpillar to turn into a butterfly. Millions of children know this book by heart, and because of it understand how a caterpillar turns into a butterfly. It's more than learning the facts; it's the story they remember.

We can support children's curiosity through story in many ways: by reading children good stories that provide facts as well as stretch the children's views of the possibilities. By encouraging children to make up their own stories, to put their sense of wonder and possibility down on paper. By allowing children to share their personal stories of their lives as much as possible—and to listen to the stories of their friends.

Stories allow us to support all three Cs in children. They use creativity to tell a good story, curiosity to drive the story and wonder what will happen next, and courtesy as they learn successful communication with others and show respect for each other by telling their own stories and listening to those of their friends.

EXPLORE THE WORLD

Another opportunity we have for supporting our children's sense of curiosity is to open the door and show them there is an entire world out there just waiting to be discovered, full of new things to learn about and explore. The more often we expose children to new places, people, and things, the more often we will pique their curiosity and get those questions flowing!

For those running schools and day cares, this means field trips. For parents, it's known as the family outing. Whatever you label it, the concept is simple—take the children outside of their typical environments and introduce them to new ones. This can mean driving somewhere, or when that's not a possibility, walking there. Go to parks, museums, zoos, fire stations, hospitals, the post office—even the local shopping mall. You'd be surprised at how exciting children find some of the simplest businesses. Consider this—a typical office (a place that seems anything but interesting to adults) is filled with things that interest children, such as chairs that spin, magazines with photos of new places, carbon paper that magically writes on a second piece of paper when you write on the first, copiers to take pictures of little hands, and so much more!

In my day care, we took a field trip every Wednesday and sometimes threw in an extra one on a great sunny day or birthday. When I closed after 17 years of business, I estimated that I had done over 900 field trips! That was 900 opportunities to show the children that there is much left to discover out there—and 900 opportunities to reestablish my own love of learning something new. Field trips were such an integral part of my program that it is no surprise to me to attend high school graduation parties for my own past graduates and hear how many of their favorite childhood memories revolve around the fieldtrips we had taken. They are some of my favorite memories as well.

My favorite field trip moment was the one we would take to the Wisconsin capitol in Madison each year for the holidays. In the rotunda, they put up an amazing tree. We enter on the ground level, walking down marbled hallways, marveling at the expanse of stone, the echo, the gold embellishments—even the light fixtures. We can see the base of the tree ahead as we walk in. The rotunda is in the middle of the building and connects the four wings. A balcony opens around it on each floor so from the top we can see all the way to the bottom—and vice versa when we stand in the middle on the ground level. We walk up to the base of the tree with a ceiling above us until those last few steps. The tree fills the circular space. The children stop, transfixed by the sparkling lights and massive branches. And then my moment: I quietly say, "Look up." All their little faces slowly tip back, looking up and up, following the tree to its very top, three stories above us, and I hear it: "Ohhhhhh."

That moment is why I became a teacher. That moment when I know I just showed the children something they never considered to exist before. That moment when I know I knocked down all those barriers they held in their minds and filled it with possibilities instead.

This is what field trips and outings can do. Even something as simple as taking a walk down the street and turning the corner to see a new street can spark the curiosity in a child. Who lives here? What are these businesses about? Why are the cows laying down? Where can you ride a bicycle here? Whenever you introduce children to something new, you are telling them that there is much out there that they don't know *yet*—but wouldn't it be great to get to know more about it?

As children get out in their world to explore, they begin to use all of their senses. Being acutely aware of input from all our senses is key in creativity, as we use this input and information to create new possibilities. But as discussed at the beginning of the chapter, creativity and curiosity are intrinsically linked, especially by the use of our senses. To pull together the information our senses gather, we must first become adept at gathering the information. Thus, it all begins with curiosity. Exploring our world through all of our senses.

This is where field trips and outings can really expand a child's mind. It's one thing to discuss how a giraffe looks by reading a book or even watching a movie. But it takes it to a new level when the child goes to a zoo, climbs the two-story platform to get up to the head of the giraffe and have it stick out that foot-long, rough blue tongue to lick up the corn in the child's outstretched palm. The sensory experiences of the sight of the giraffe's height, the smell of its breath, the touch of its tongue all meld together to build an entirely new level of understanding of a giraffe. As children explore the world firsthand through these sensory experiences, they build a firm foundation for gathering information and using it later in creative and imaginative ways.

Get children outside to see the world, but do more than just take them from one building (their home or school) into another building (a museum or fire station). Show them what the world is truly *made* of: nature. Get them into the woods, out in the meadows, near the lakes and streams. Help them to build an appreciation and sense of wonder of the beauty of nature. Nature holds many secrets for children to explore and become curious about, and all of it is overflowing with sensory experiences.

Richard Louv (2005) found in his research that even though children felt a disconnect with nature, it did not mean that they lacked curiosity about it. He writes: "These kids spoke of nature with a strange mixture of puzzlement, detachment, and yearning—and occasional defiance" (p. 13).

As discussed in the creativity chapter, Louv (2005) points out that the availability of nature for children has become almost nonexistent. "Parents, educators, other adults, institutions—the culture itself—may say one thing to children about nature's gifts, but so many of our actions and messages—especially the ones we cannot hear ourselves deliver—are different. And children hear very well" (p. 14). He states that the regulatory message is clear: "Islands of nature that are left by the graders are to be seen, not touched" (p. 43).

Louv (2005) states that safety is one of the factors that contribute to this change of attitude in adults toward children's involvement with nature. In our quest to keep our children safe, we have removed many of the variables that allowed children to follow their natural curiosity through nature. I experienced this myself with a few neighbors. I had a small crabapple tree in my front yard. The entire tree stood only about 12 feet tall, and it had many horizontal low branches perfect for climbing. I encouraged my day care children to climb, always allowing them to follow their natural abilities and curiosities regarding how high they went. I did not help a child to climb higher; it was through their own development that they would become able to reach and climb to the next branch and prove their ability. On one particular occasion, two children were on fairly low branches (approximately three to four feet off the ground) and one older child had proudly made it to a higher branch (about six feet off the ground). In just over 10 minutes, two different neighbors passed by on walks and stopped to comment. Both were furious with me for letting the children climb the tree, citing it as "dangerous" and "unsafe" and voicing concern for the children's safety. I assured each that the children were only climbing as high as they had the capability for and that because of this were quite safe. Neither neighbor was appeased and both left upset with me. Because of their visits, I questioned the activity myself and later talked with the parents about it. I was relieved to hear that they also valued the curiosity of their children and their ability to try something new and push their development to reach new places—literally. I continued the practice and tend to climb a tree myself now and then!

Gerry Slater (2008), from Playworks4Kids, designs and builds innovative, high-quality play environments for children. His response to the pressure on early childhood teachers to get children ready for school is, "Real learning goes far beyond scoring well in academic tests or being school-ready. Thoughtful, intentional early childhood educators can provide outdoor experiences and activities that respond to virtually all the developmental learning tasks facing young children" (p. 13).

He recommends that the focus of early childhood education be "supporting children's sense of wonder and curiosity as they develop an appreciation for and love of the natural world" (Slater, 2008, p. 13).

Giving children the opportunity to explore nature and their world can best be accomplished by combining the experiences of being out in the world with experiences at home and school that bring the outside world in. Just as we discussed supporting creativity through the child's environment, we should do so with curiosity in mind as well. The key is in organizing the space so that materials will actually be used and explored. Consider the children's abilities and interests and provide them materials in ways that interest them and challenge them developmentally. Materials that encourage exploration through a variety of senses will keep a curious child content and ready to learn. (See the activities in the following chapter for specific ideas.)

In addition to bringing items into the classroom and home for the children to explore, bring in the people they may encounter in the world as well! Invite speakers to share their passions: artists, scientists, zoo workers, and so on. Show the children there are many interesting things happening and curious people who are attempting new and exciting things. Encourage the children to ask lots of questions during these visits to push their curiosity and wonder all they can in order to learn all they can.

Another great avenue for supporting a child's curiosity is through dress-up play. Children are very curious about adults, the roles they play, the jobs they have. They love to explore these worlds through play. They can create their own what-if scenarios and be part of the answers they explore. It helps them to learn through hands-on experience how to problem solve. Curiosity leads children into exploring what they see and what they know, such as putting on a baker's hat and a police officer's costume, and perhaps baking a cake and helping someone who is lost. But through play, this curiosity evolves past what the children know into what they can imagine—bringing them into a creative process. The baker decides to bake a cake using some concrete freshly poured into the sidewalk; the police officer steps into the concrete to stop him and gets stuck. It is this back and forth between curiosity and creativity that moves a child's play forward and leads to problem solving. The baker discovers that when he mixed the sugar with the concrete, it no longer would get hard, so he adds sugar to the concrete the police officer has stepped into. It softens and he can now get out! The role-playing aspect of dress-up play allows children to look beyond themselves and how they would react to a situation and consider how someone else may see it. This also increases their sense of empathy, which falls under our third C, courtesy. Dress-up play is one of the activities that can encompass the three Cs while exploring the concept that the teacher or parent would like to see explored. All it takes is a few of the right props, and the children can take it from there.

ASK QUESTIONS: THE FIVE WS AND HOW

To encourage the inquisitive nature of children, we can take opportunities to ask them questions as a means to move them toward self-motivated learning and exploration. In posing questions to children that push their limits and move them into a curious state, go beyond the obvious. Think about the details and see where it leads the child by using the "five Ws and how" that journalists depend on: who, what, where, when, why, and how. For example, when looking at animals, rather than asking which are farm animals and which are wild, ask the child what differences they see in the animals' tails. Break things down into small details; there are many in every subject we teach. Children love to take the time to notice these things and are very good at finding the ones we may have overlooked.

Also, keep in mind the type of questions you ask. If they are factual, they will have only one answer. If they are interpretive, the answers will vary and can be numerous. For example, asking a group of children how a certain color makes them feel will give you a much deeper discussion than asking them which children are wearing that color.

Another form of questioning is called the "Socratic method." The great philosopher Socrates used this technique to guide others toward their own insights. It simply means that questions are answered with more questions. It is a valuable tool for parents and teachers to open up their children's minds and inspire deeper thought.

One of the simplest forms of questioning is simply to ask, "What if . . ." and state something out of the ordinary for the child to consider. Show them through this modeling that it is useful and fun to consider something unknown or surprising or different from the norm. Pick an item, such as a horse. Model for the children by saying, "What if a horse knocked on the door and said he wanted to come to school today?" This can lead to a very in-depth and animated discussion! Then turn it over to the children, asking them to consider something new. Their what-if scenarios will illustrate for you the depths of their curiosity.

And finally, there is the old standby, the one word children learn almost as soon as they speak and never seem to stop using: "Why?" Nothing encapsulates curiosity better than this simple word. It should be something we hear often, encourage to hear even more, and when we do hear it, take action. Not just by providing a simple, closed-ended answer but by acknowledging that the word opens a door to possibilities to be explored with joy and wonder. When children ask "why," it is our cue to guide them to (not provide them) an answer. Our direct answer should be, "Let's find out!" And then to take that journey together.

A great way to take journeys together through new experiences and learning is to engage the children in projects—the creation of something that involves investigation, problem solving, and creativity that is driven by the children's curiosity.

Judy Harris Helm (2008), author of seven books on the project approach, tells us that "even in classrooms in which standards and required curriculum are prominent, there is still a place for rich, integrated learning experiences that truly engage children, such as projects" (p. 14). She maintains that "when children are engaged they are excited, curious, and intensely involved in learning experiences that are meaningful to them" (p. 14). For this reason, engagement becomes a valid criterion for selecting learning experiences.

The project approach greatly supports this engagement. At its foundation is the expectation that children will follow their natural curiosity toward further learning. This approach not only supports curiosity, it also supports the children passing many other developmental

Books on the Project Approach

The Project Approach: Making Curriculum Come Alive by Sylvia Chard (1998). New York: Scholastic Teaching Resources.

Young Investigators: The Project Approach in the Early Years by Judy Harris Helm and Lilian Katz (2000). New York: Teachers College Press.

Engaging Children's Minds: The Project Approach, Second Edition by Lilian G. Katz and Sylvia C. Chard (2000). New York: Ablex.

milestones on their journey, opening the door for teachers to meet many of their curriculum goals. Information on conducting a project can be found in books by Judy Harris Helm and others. (See sidebar.)

In addition to the project approach, constructive play also supports the core of curiosity, leading to further learning. Constructive play is defined as "building and making things no one has ever seen before" (Drew, Christie, Johnson, Meckley, & Nell, 2008, p. 38). In *Constructive Play: A Value-Added Strategy for Meeting Early Learning Standards*, these authors report that "as young children fiddle with, sort, and arrange materials, ideas and imagination begin to flow" (p. 38). The act of working constructively leads to natural curiosity and wonder. "In this way, constructive play serves to focus the minds of children through their fingertips and leads them to invent and discover new possibilities, to fulfill their sense of purpose" (p. 38).

Based on the authors' collective work as play researchers and teacher educators, they explain why developmentally appropriate constructive play is an ideal instructional strategy for meeting early learning standards: "During the preschool years, constructive play merges with exploration and make-believe play and becomes a mature form of play that allows children to strengthen inquiry skills and build conceptual understanding" (Drew et al., 2008, p. 39).

Constructive play, together with projects, dress-up play, an open atmosphere for questioning, opportunities to explore both in classrooms and homes as well as out in the real world and in nature, plus an overriding sense of wonder, excitement about the possibilities, and desire to be a scientist, a dreamer, a storyteller, will give your children the foundation of curiosity to serve them in their further learning.

Curiosity can lead us in many directions. Because of this, spontaneity is essential for the adults supporting a child's natural curiosity. Being able to switch gears and discuss what a child's interest is in, rather than force a conversation on

Children's Books That Spark Curiosity

The Quiet Noisy Book by Margaret Wise Brown (1993). New York: HarperCollins.

Hailstones and Halibut Bones by Mary O'Neil (1961). New York: Delacorte Press.

Inventors by Martin Sandler (1999). New York: HarperCollins.

Usborne Farmyard Tales Children's Cookbook by Fiona Watt and Stephen Cartwright, illustrated by Molly Sage (2003). London: Usborne Books.

Curious George by H. A. Rey (1941). New York: Houghton Mifflin.

Fancy Nancy, Explorer Extraordinaire! by Jane O'Connor and Robin Preiss Glasser (2009). New York: HarperCollins.

The Berenstain Bears and the Spooky Old Tree by Stan and Jan Berenstain (1978). New York: Random House.

a predisposed topic, will enable children to grow and learn through their curiosity. To do this, teachers and parents can remember that their job in supporting their children's development is to look at the big picture, to focus on the *concepts* they would like their children to learn, not the *topics*. For example, if the concept you would like to teach is about items being "big, bigger, biggest," and you've picked the topic of apples to illustrate this, but your child comes to you full of questions about birds—keep the concept, but change the topic. Help your child explore books and toys to find three birds that he or she can use to represent "big, bigger, biggest." Lesson learned. Curiosity intact.

We've all heard the saying "give a man a fish and he eats for a day; teach him to fish and he eats for a lifetime." This saying encompasses the impact of curiosity on human life. A man can simply accept a fish, or he can ask, "How did you catch it?" If we teach our children facts, they will have information, but if we teach our children to explore the facts, they will have the power to change the world.

Curiosity Activities 5

Children are naturally curious, so to be sure this sense of exploration doesn't get lost in your day, give them lots of opportunities to follow their own questions and be exposed to new things, people, and experiences that build their interest. By supporting a strong curiosity, parents and teachers are giving children the tools to construct their own learning, to make it more meaningful, and to have more success in school. The following categories naturally allow children to follow and build their sense of creativity: exploring the possibilities through wonder, experimentation, and story; exploring our world through field trips and dramatic play; and asking all the questions—the "five Ws and how"—who, what where, when, why, and how. Activities under each of these areas will be listed under one of the two state standards most often met through curiosity activities: science or language and literacy. Because curiosity activities often include gathering data or asking and answering questions, these two areas are well covered by adding curiosity to your curriculum.

EXPLORE THE POSSIBILITIES

Language and Literature

STORYTELLER FUN

Professional storytellers make even the simplest stories come alive. Either take a field trip to visit them or invite them to your classroom. In addition to having the storytellers tell stories, have the children prepare questions to ask the storytellers about what they do and how they learned to do it. After the visit, have the children choose one of their favorite stories and do a storytelling session on it for the group. *Activity supports curiosity through story and encourages creativity as children learn a variety of ways to tell a story.*

NEWSPAPER NAMES

Give the children a highlighter marker and a story cut from a newspaper. Ask the children to look closely at the words on their pages and highlight all the letters they can find from their names. This gets children more curious about the written word in other forms, such as the newspaper they see their parents read. *Activity supports curiosity through exploration of possibilities as children discover new forms of the written word.*

STORY MIXER

Read two different storybooks to the children. Make a list of the characters from one story and the setting and plot from another story. Then mix the two together! With the children, write a new story using the mixed-up items. Would the characters act differently than in the original story? What would they do? How would they react to the problem? Would it change the ending? Have the children draw new illustrations to go with it and create a new class book. *Activity supports curiosity by exploring the possibilities in a story when small changes are made as children experiment and wonder; activity also supports creativity through stimulus freedom.*

UPPER- AND LOWERCASE MATCH GAME

Buy paper cut into two different shapes, such as frogs and fish, or use a die cutter. Write capital letters on one shape, one per paper, and lowercase letters on the other shape, one per paper. Laminate or cover with clear contact paper to make them sturdier if you like. Give one child, or two who can work together, the shapes, mixed up. First, have the children spread them all out so they can see them, with all of one shape in one area and all of the other shape in another area. Ask them to pick up a letter (such as a capital *A* on a fish), and then find the matching lowercase letter (such as a lowercase *a* on a frog). Encourage discussion about the commonalities and differences between the upper- and lowercase letters. Some are the same, some are slightly different, some are very different. You can have the children sort them into these three categories as they find the matches, counting how many sets end up in each group. Encourages close observation skills and letter recognition. *Activity supports curiosity through wonder and experimentation as children work to find correct matches.*

WHERE IS TOMMY?

Create index cards, or fun shapes, with each letter of the children's names on a separate card. Hide the letters around the room while the children are not there. When they arrive, tell them that their names are hidden in the room and they must now go find them, like playing hide and seek with themselves! Don't worry if several children share a letter—as long as there is a card for each, it won't matter which one they find. When a child finds all his or her letters, have the child line up the cards on a table in the correct order and then help a friend. *Encourages curiosity as children wonder where their names could be, supports letter recognition, and helps support courtesy as they learn to help each other.*

Science

EXPLORING THE SOUND OF . . . PAPER!

Give each child a sheet of paper. It can be any kind—construction, newspaper, typing paper, poster board, or tissue paper. Ask them to see how many different sounds they can make with it. They can crumble it. Rip it. Tap it against itself. Blow on it or wave it. Let them try to come up with something you haven't discovered. *Activity supports curiosity through the exploration of possibilities with the senses and also supports creativity through functional freedom, using paper for something other than drawing on.*

RECIPE CARDS

Provide each child a copy of a recipe. Create them using a standard sheet of paper and draw (or use photos of) the ingredients for the recipe, writing the name of the ingredient next to it. Or you can draw it on a large chalkboard or dry erase board. Also include the measurements, such as "¼ cup," "1 cup," "2 teaspoons," and so on. Don't abbreviate—write out the entire word. Go over the recipe with the children, helping them to read it on their own. When making the recipes, use one they may have some familiarity with, such as chocolate chip cookies. Add a couple of ingredients in the recipe that do not belong, such as "2 cups pickles" or "1 cup bacon." After reading all the ingredients, talk with the children about what may be wrong in the recipe. Have them point out the items and read them aloud. Talk about the measurements and if they seem correct. You can put in a few that will need to be changed, such as "1 cup salt" or "5 bags chocolate chips." (Although they may vote to leave in that much chocolate!) After the discussion about reading the recipe and understanding it thoroughly, shift the lesson to hands-on learning by making the cookies. Encourage the children to find the ingredients by reading the labels of items in the cupboard and to find the sizes marked on measuring tools. *Activity supports curiosity through experimentation with ingredients in a recipe and also supports literacy development.*

HOT OR COLD?

Put out four glasses of the same size. Fill each with water—but vary the temperature of the water in each. For example, fill the first cup all the way with very hot water (hot to the touch, but not so hot it burns), fill the next cup half full, and fill the next cup a quarter full. Add cold water to fill all of these, and fill the last glass with the cold water. Have the children dip their fingers into each glass to determine the temperature, and then ask them to line up the glasses, hottest to coldest. Explores the sense of touch using temperature. *Activity supports curiosity as it raises a child's sense of wonder and allows for experimentation.*

CREATE A TEXTURE BOOK

Texture books are often used for infants to explore, but older children can benefit from this tactile experience as well. Create a texture book for them to explore and discuss. Create a simple book using construction paper stapled on the binding (cover the staples with masking or duct tape to prevent scratches). On each page, glue a tactile item, such as tinfoil, cotton balls, sandpaper, plastic sandwich bag, cloth, imitation fur, felt, corrugated cardboard, feathers, and so on. Allow children time to explore the touch of each and discuss why each feels the way it does. Have children close their eyes and see if they can identify a page using only their sense of touch. *Activity supports curiosity by using the senses to wonder and explore.*

WIND CHIMES

Create wind chimes with the children to explore different sounds. Cut a four-inch circle from heavy cardboard. Punch four to six holes around it and tie strings to the holes. Each string should be one to two feet long. Punch two holes close together in the middle of the circle and tie a two-foot-long string to it so it hangs down from the middle of the circle. Tie a two-inch-wide metal washer to the end of the middle string. Next, tie another string to the middle that will be used on the top to hang the chime. Then collect items for the chime that when bumped against the washer will produce a sound, such as washers of different sizes, pieces of PVC pipe, large nails or screws, or any small metal toy. Tie them onto the side strings so they hang at the same level as the washer in the middle (so they can bump it to make sounds). Experiment with the different items to hear the different sounds they create—both alone and together. Make different chimes and discuss the differences in the sounds they make. *Activity supports curiosity through experimentation as children work to find different sounds for the chimes.*

CREATING RECIPES

Cooking is a fantastic activity for inspiring a child's curiosity and thinking. Encourage the children to create their own recipes. Provide a variety of ingredients and tools for the children to use, and allow them to experiment. Set out items that would typically go together for a certain type of cooking, such as flour, sugar, butter, and eggs for baking. Or meat, canned soup, vegetables, and cheese for an entrée. You may want to add one item from an opposite product group just to allow them to experiment with the results, such as putting in a bowl of cut carrots with the baking ingredients. Give the children bowls, spoons, measuring cups, rolling pins, whisks, and other utensils to work with. Have the children record their recipe on a card as they create it (adding some literacy work). For nonwriters, create cards with drawings or photos of ingredients that the children pick up when they choose that ingredient. Have them keep the cards together as they create their recipe. You can even put checkboxes on each card next to drawings of quarter-, half-, and one-cup measuring cups so they can simply check off the size they used for that ingredient. When they have finished any mixing, let them decide how the food is to be cooked: baked on a sheet or in a pan, cooked in a bowl in a microwave oven, or fried in a skillet. Help them to follow through on their recipe to the end and taste the results. Then they can add a smiley face or sad face sticker to their recipe card, showing how it turned out. For those that do not turn out well—remember there's no using the word *can't!*—help the children look over their recipe and decide what might need to be changed so next time they can try it with the changes. Cooking is experimental science at its best—help the children learn through trial and error, follow their natural curiosities about ingredients and how they interact, and you may have the next five-star chef on your hands! *Activity supports curiosity through experimentation and wonder as well as using the senses of touch, smell, sight, and taste.*

THE KEYS TO CURIOSITY

Provide the children with a basketful of keys. Your local hardware store should be able to provide them at no cost; they often save keys that were cut wrong. Use the keys as a conversation starter. Allow the children to pick keys from the basket. Ask them, "What do you think that key opens?"

Engage in conversation about all the possibilities. Children may even wish to try the keys in different locks around your room—support this curiosity. *Activity supports curiosity through wonder of the possibilities.*

EXPLORE THE WORLD

Language and Literacy

LETTER COLLECTION

This activity can be done inside or out or both. Choose a letter, and ask the children to collect items they see that begin with that letter. Give them baskets or buckets to put their collections in as they search. Also give them flashlights, magnifying glasses, binoculars, or other "explorer gear" to get them in the spirit of the hunt. You can do this over time, such as an hour, day, or week. Or you can make it a race and give them only minutes. Once items have been collected, have the children share what they found with the group, passing them around for close inspection. Write the names of the items on a chalkboard or dry erase board, and display the items for further exploration on a table near the written list. You can also write the names on index cards and let the children match the words to the correct items. *Activity supports curiosity as children connect letters to the world around them and search for the possibilities.*

Science

DISCOVERY CORNER

Provide the children an area in the room for exploration and discovery. Display items for investigation on shelves, rather than in baskets, to pique interest. For example, a large seashell on one shelf alone, three small pinecones on another shelf, and a large rock broken into two pieces on another. Change items often to keep them curious about what may show up there. Also include items that can be taken apart and explored, such as old toasters or radios. Include either a sensory table (a large tub) or individual tubs for sensory play and discovery. Offer a variety of mediums, such as sand, water, rice, or pasta, rotating them often. Consider mixing mediums together. Provide a shelf or table for ongoing experiments, such as three plants to explore how water affects them—water one each day, overwater another, and don't water the third for a week to see which grows best. Provide items that help them explore with a variety of senses, such as three glasses of different liquids with different smells, a tape recorder with tapes of animal or nature sounds to identify, and so on. This is a good area to keep a pet in for observation. Have a couple of "Explorer Kits" in the area as well (see instructions below). *Area supports curiosity through exploration of new items from the world around the children and the possibilities of experimentation.*

EXPLORER KIT

Every good explorer needs the right tools for discovery. Provide a few of these kits in your discovery area, and create extras for taking outside. In the outside kits, include a compass and binoculars. Make the kits using either fanny packs, small shoulder bags, or metal lunchboxes, preferably with a camouflage design. Make it fun for the children to dress up as real explorers, and they'll be more excited about trying out the discovery area.

Contents to include:

Magnifying glass—several types and sizes

Stethoscope

Tweezers

Small clear plastic jars

Petri dishes

Magnet

Small notepad and pencil

Small plastic jar of water and eyedropper (to observe how items change when wet)

Small cloth for drying objects

Handheld tape recorder to tape sounds made with objects

Color paddles

Prism

Small flashlight

Safety goggles

An explorer's kit supports curiosity by giving children the tools they need to explore their world, experiment, and wonder.

ME AND MY SHADOW

In the morning of a sunny day, have the children stand on a driveway or paved playground area to cast shadows of themselves. Use sidewalk chalk to trace the shadows. Let the children use the chalk to finish the drawings by adding eyes, hair, clothes, and so on. Then, a couple hours later, have them return to the spot to see if they can repeat the shadows. The sun will have moved, and their shadows will have moved too. Let them each trace another outline. Continue this throughout the day to see just where the shadows travel to. *Activity supports curiosity through exploration of our world, the sun and its shadows, the turning of the earth, and our place in it all.*

SMELLY DAY FOR A WALK!

Take a walk outside with the children and stop at intervals to close your eyes and smell. Have the children do this as well and see what smells they can discover. Stop often to smell things, such as flowers, tree bark, mud, garbage, a puddle, a dog pen, and so on. Make a list of the smells so when you return inside you can discuss them again. *Activity supports curiosity through exploration of the outdoors, heightening awareness of the sense of smell.*

SOUND BINGO

Create your own sound bingo game by using a tape recorder to record a variety of sounds, such as children laughing, a baby crying, a dog barking, a door slamming, water running, and so on. A second or two after each sound, state the name of the sound into the recorder as well. Then create bingo boards of the sounds using pictures of the items you find on the Internet. Give the children small cars or other toys to place over the photos as bingo chips. Play the tape and see how many sounds they can find on their boards. When you play a sound, stop the recorder immediately and see if everyone can figure out what the sound is before you reveal it by restarting the tape. *Activity supports curiosity through exploration of the world while focusing on the sense of hearing.*

SMELL JARS

Collect six to eight plastic film canisters. Poke holes in the top of each. Inside, place items with strong smells such as coffee, cinnamon, pepper. Or place a cotton ball inside and pour a little extract on it, such as peppermint, vanilla, or cherry. Replace the lids. Make two jars for each scent. Mix the canisters together and see if the children can match the scents. *Activity supports curiosity through exploration of the world around us, the possibilities in the sense of smell, and the possibilities of matches.*

DINOSAUR DIG

Children are fascinated by dinosaurs—they love to play with toy dinosaurs, read dinosaur books, and sing dinosaur songs. But to help your children grasp a more concrete understanding of a scientist's discovery of dinosaurs, create your own dinosaur bones for the children to uncover!

Wet the sand in a sandbox and use shovels and other tools to carve out a large dinosaur bone mold, preferably at least three feet long. Look at dinosaur books to get ideas about what shapes to make. Line the mold with the heavy plastic found in the painting departments of local hardware stores and at construction sites (it's used to cover the insulation in houses before siding is applied). You will need a five-gallon bucket (or wheelbarrow) and bags of cement. Read the instructions on the bag to determine the quantity you will need for the size bone you are creating. Mix cement and water until it looks like runny oatmeal. Pour into mold and let sit overnight to dry. Once dry, you can paint the bones using cement paint if you like but, the gray color of concrete works well too. (Or you can mix concrete stains with the concrete while it's wet.) Make a large variety of bones in different sizes and shapes. Bury the bones in the sandbox, covering them completely. Or you can hide the bones in large piles of leaves.

Offer the children a variety of brushes, large and small, and show them how paleontologists uncover bones without harming them by brushing softly. Then let the children discover the bones. Seeing the large bones will help make it more real to them just how big dinosaurs were, especially if you explain to them that the three-foot piece is just one toe! *Activity supports curiosity as children become interested in dinosaurs and engage in hands-on activity to follow their natural curiosities, exploring a world where dinosaurs exist.*

SOUND WALK

Take a walk outdoors with the children. Stop at the beginning and listen. Ask the children what sound they hear first, name it (such as "dog barking"), and write it down. Continue the walk, stopping occasionally to ask the children what they hear and writing it down. At the end of the walk, stop and ask what the last sound they hear is. When you return to the classroom or house, ask the children what the first and last sounds were that they heard. Show them your written list to see if they are right. Read the list from first sound to last. This activity helps children learn the basis for phonetic awareness as they learn to pay attention to the beginning and end sounds in words. Teachers and parents can move directly from this activity to a phonetic activity that discusses beginning and end sounds of words. *Activity supports curiosity through exploration of the sounds of our world as well as the possibilities of sounds and letters.*

TERRARIUMS

Help the children create their own terrariums in order to closely observe the growth of plants. Cut off three to four inches from the bottom of a clear plastic drink bottle. Fill the bottom with soil and sprinkle with seeds, being sure to place some seeds against the sides so the children will be able to see the roots as they grow against the side of the bottle. Spray generously with water. Replace the top of the bottle and tape back together. Screw the lid on as well. Daily, unscrew the lid and spray water into the bottle, replacing the lid. Have the children observe the bottles daily and discuss what they see. Also have them predict how many days they think it will be before they see growth from their seeds, or how many days until their plant has grown one inch high. *Activity supports curiosity through exploration of plants and the environments they need to grow.*

ASK QUESTIONS

Language and Literacy

TODAY, I AM INTERVIEWING . . .

Set up a video camera and create a newsroom set. Choose a child to be interviewed—this is a great activity for a child's birthday or first day of school. Now choose a couple other children to be the interviewers. Give them play microphones, press passes, bowler hats, vests, and so on to get them in the spirit. You can also make a child a camera operator or producer. Give the children ideas on what types of questions to ask, and let them conduct an interview with the special child. If you like, you can have the children take turns so everyone gets a chance in each role or make it a tradition for a birthday child to be interviewed, giving the tape to the parents as a special keepsake of their child's birthday. *Activity supports curiosity as children learn to both ask and answer a variety of questions and learn how simple questions can lead to an infusion of new information.*

MORE THAN JUST THE FACTS

Present the children with a fact of some kind that ties into a topic you are discussing, such as the number of pandas in the world. Or in fall, that a maple tree's leaves turn red and yellow. Then encourage the children to find the story that hides behind the fact. What is the story of the panda? When and where were they first found? Why are there so few? What is the most there ever were? The idea is to spark their curiosity about a topic by giving them a fact and having them look into why that fact is true. Provide books, films, field trips, guest speakers, dramatic play materials, art supplies, and other items to help them explore the topic and find their story. Tell the children they are to act like sleuth reporters looking for the story behind the facts. When they have information for a story, help them create it by acting it out or creating a book or song about it. *Activity supports curiosity as children consider questions, and then learn the techniques and tools needed to find answers to their questions on any topic.*

Activity alternative: Provide the children with a photograph of something. It can be an animal, a person, or a place, something simple, or an intriguing scene. Ask them to look closely at the photo and to make up a story based on what they see. You can help them write the story down. They can also draw new scenes to add to their story, using the photo for the cover.

WHAT I SEE . . .

Pass around an object among the children, such as a teddy bear, and ask them to investigate it closely and try to notice as many details about it as they can. Then ask each child to share a remembered detail, writing each answer down on a chalkboard or on paper for the children to see. Talk with the children about how these are "descriptive" words—they are used to describe what we see. Read them over again. Then, pointing to one word at a time, ask them if they can name something else they could use the same descriptive word for, such as *furry* for the teddy bear as well as a pet rabbit. *Activity teaches an understanding of the specific use of a category of words and encourages curiosity regarding details of an object.*

FROM ONE LIBRARY TO ANOTHER

While not a specific activity for the children, creating your own library of reference materials for their use is important in supporting their curiosity. Most local libraries have monthly book sales—a great opportunity for gathering large quantities of books. They also will often have reference book sets, perfect for your little explorers. Try to get books with photos about animals, places, people, transportation, food, and other topics they can use when creating stories or doing research. *Enhancing a library supports curiosity as children learn to turn to books for answers to their many questions.*

WHAT I REALLY WANT TO KNOW

Pair children together and ask each to choose a favorite toy from the room or use a special item brought from home. While sitting together, encourage each child to come up with three questions to ask a friend about the item the friend has. For younger children, you may wish to model this by doing the activity with a child yourself. Encourage the children to ask questions using the five Ws and how. Help them be creative with their questions, such as "Have you ever taken a bath with that book?" or "Is that the car your pet gerbil drives?" For older children, you can write these prompts on a chalkboard to help guide them. Also, encourage the children to think of questions that involve their senses—how does it feel, smell, sound, taste, look? Again, post these prompts for older children. Allow these question-and-answer sessions to grow into natural conversations between the children. *Activity supports curiosity as children see that they can ask any question they have, and that there are no "bad" questions.*

Science

TASTING PARTY

Obtain a large selection of foods for the children to explore. Present them one at a time at first; discuss how they affect each of the five senses. How does it look—is it large or small? What color is it? How does it feel—hard, soft, scratchy, furry? How does it smell—sweet, tart, no smell, woodsy? If you shake it, do you hear anything? If you rub it or squeeze it, what does it sound like? And finally, how does it taste? Also, once they are eating it—how does it feel on their tongues? After exploring several items, have the children begin to put them together by similarities—perhaps all the hard ones together or the ones that make noise. Try to find a similarity other than color—get creative! *Activity supports curiosity as children explore new foods in more ways than only taste by asking questions about the food to expand their knowledge.*

WHAT'S HIDING HERE?

When the children can't see you, lay out several scarves on the floor or table. Place random items under the scarves, such as a cup, roll of toilet paper (with the paper still on), pinecone, ball, marker, stuffed animal, hat, pan, soap dispenser, toy car, and so on. Start with just five or six objects. Have each child look over the "bump" created by the object under the scarf and guess what it is—without touching. Then, let the child touch the object through the scarf and guess again. Finally, pull off the scarf to see what was hidden. During the activity, increase their curiosity by asking questions. Which object sticks up the highest? Who sees one you are sure you know? Which object is the biggest? The smallest? Which one feels soft? And so on. *Activity supports curiosity as children explore objects in a new way, heightening their interest because the objects are at first unseen and then allowing for further exploration of their details through questioning.*

Activity extenders: Use the activity to also promote literacy by giving each child a chart to write down guesses during each step. Create rows for "Look only," "Touch," and "See." The children can then graph how many they had right in each category.

For younger children, create cards with photos or drawings of each of the objects and have them lay them in front of the hidden object they believe it matches. This also makes it into a math activity.

POP! GOES THE ANSWER!

Place a hot-air popcorn popper on the floor in an area big enough for the children to gather around. Pour in the popcorn—but do not put the top on. Have the children gather around, staying far enough back so they don't touch the popper. Talk with the children about what happens when you turn on a popcorn popper—it gets hot and the kernels burst. Explain how the moisture in the kernel gets hot and pushes open the hard shell, making the "pop!" Turn on the machine. Ask the children what they think will happen when the corn begins to pop without the lid on. Where will it go? Will it still stay in the popper? Will it go up in the air? How high do they think it will go? Will they be able to catch it? Continue the questions as the anticipation grows and they wait for those first pops. When it does begin to pop, talk about what changes from the first few pops to when it gets popping really fast. (The first few kernels may fly out, but once the machine begins to fill, it should just overflow without kernels flying.) When the popcorn is done, turn off the popper and talk about if it did what the children anticipated it would do. Then glue the popped corn onto paper to make an art project. (Warning: Do not give popcorn to children to eat because it is a choking hazard for children under five years old.) *Activity supports curiosity as children consider the many questions and possibilities and become invested in following through on the experiment to find the answers. Activity also supports creativity through delayed gratification.*

Integrating Curiosity Activities

6

Just as creativity and curiosity are intrinsically linked in problem solving, curiosity is imbedded in much of the learning that children do. Their natural curiosity leads them to explore, experiment, and ask questions. Teachers and parents wishing to protect this natural instinct need only fill the children's days with possibilities and be ready to follow their questions. Creating activities that meet early learning standards does not mean forgetting curiosity; it is possible to integrate the two. As you create activities in the standard areas, take the time to instill them with possibilities, stray away from activities that have only one outcome, and look to expand activities to follow the questions and curiosities of the children as they participate. This chapter will focus on how we can create these experiences to meet standards in other categories.

MATH

SAME VERSUS DIFFERENT

Collect photos of animals of similar types but different species, such as a rattlesnake and cobra, a black bear and polar bear, and a parrot and sparrow. Give them to the children in pairs and talk about what is the same and what is different about the animals in the set. Help the children to really look at the details of the colorings, the sizes, the shapes, the eyes, and so on. Notice the differences yet recognize why they are the same type of animal. *Activity helps support curiosity through sensory exploration (visual) and supports math standards through comparison and contrast.*

HEAVY VERSUS LIGHT

Collect buckets with lids, such as ice-cream cartons. Try to get at least five. Cover the buckets and lids with solid-colored contact paper so the children can't see what's inside. (Cover the buckets separately from the lids so you can remove them.) Fill each bucket with water to a different level. Put on the lids. Arrange the buckets in no particular order. Ask a child to pick up each bucket and consider its weight. By picking up two at a time, the child becomes a scale and determines which of the two is heavier. Have the child place the heaviest to the right, lightest to the left. Then give the child another bucket and by holding that bucket and one of the first two, determine where it fits in the lineup—is it heavier or lighter? Continue this comparison until the child thinks all the buckets are arranged from lightest to heaviest. Then remove the covers to compare the water levels to see if the child was right. This activity can be done individually or in small groups by taking turns or working together with each comparison. Encourage discussion during the activity about weight—what they think is in the buckets, which buckets they guess will be heaviest before picking them up, and so on. *Activity supports curiosity through exploration of the sense of weight and the experimentation of comparisons while supporting math development through comparisons and an understanding of weight.*

MARY, MARY, QUITE CONTRARY, HOW DOES YOUR GARDEN GROW?

Growing a garden with children brings out their curiosity as well as supporting many areas of development. Here we focus on math development. When planting a garden, pour the contents of each packet of seeds into a small paper cup and tape the packet to the outside of the cup. Have the children explore the seeds with magnifying glasses for a while and notice the differences and similarities. Then ask the children to sort the seeds by size, lining up the cups in order from the smallest seeds to the largest. Next, have them arrange the cups by grouping the same types of foods or flowers the seeds will become—for example, vegetables in one group and flowers in another or types of beans, types of tomatoes, types of melons, and so on. Then, after they have grown their garden, you can spend a day harvesting and again do categorizing, placing the same types of items together or the same sizes or the same colors. *Activity supports curiosity through exploration of seeds and experimentation of growth patterns while supporting math activity through comparisons and classification.*

PEOPLE COME IN ALL SHAPES AND SIZES

Using yarn, have the children measure each other's height. One child can lie down while another unrolls the yarn to measure his or her length. They can measure from feet to top of head, or extend their arms above their heads and measure from feet to tips of fingers. Use a different color yarn for each child. After each is measured, lay the yarns down on the floor side-by-side to see which is longest. This activity may be repeated by measuring different body parts—an arm, the crown of the head, a leg, a finger, a nose, and so on. *Activity supports curiosity through comparisons, exploration of body parts, and experimentation while also supporting creativity through functional freedom of yarn being used as a measuring tape, and math development through measurement.*

STAR LIGHT, STAR BRIGHT

This activity connects home and school nicely. Talk with the children about the stars in the night sky—what they think about them and how many they see. Ask them to spend time that night with their parents outside looking at the stars—and try counting them! Ask the parents to participate and write down their child's guess. The next day, have the children share what they saw and encourage their statements of wonder—how far away they are, how many there are, if anyone else lives out there, and if they will ever get to visit one in a spaceship. Compare the numbers they bring in. Have books available for the children to look through to get more information about stars. Read sections to them, show them pictures, take all their questions seriously, and follow through to help them find the answers. End this by giving them art materials to make pictures of the stars. *Activity supports curiosity by presenting children with something in our world they know little about and allowing them the opportunity to wonder before searching for information and using the new information to lead them to yet more wondering. Activity also supports math development through number comparison.*

Activity extender: This activity can be done in the same manner for any kind of item there are many of in our world, such as clouds, ants, birds, clovers, and so on. First encourage them to wonder, and then give them an opportunity to experience and interact with the subject, show them how to find answers, and let the answers lead them to even more wonder and exploration.

SHAVING CREAM EXPERIMENT

Fill three very large bowls with shaving cream, and then squirt in some liquid watercolor—a primary color in each bowl: red, blue, and yellow.

Have the children mix the watercolor well with the shaving cream. Then, on the table in front of each child, glob a heaping spoonful of red shaving cream and one of yellow, and have the children smush the two creams together. Do the same with blue and yellow and then red and blue. Once they have the three new colors (orange, green, and purple), let them begin their own mixing and experimenting with color combinations. Encourage them to try a larger proportion of one color with a small proportion of a second to see how it changes the outcome. *Activity supports creativity through experimentation and sensory exploration while supporting math development through an understanding of color.*

MATH STORY

Give the children a variety of stickers and 10 sheets of paper. Have them put one sticker on one page, two on a second, three on a third, and so on through 10. Each page should have the same kind of stickers (two frog stickers, three chicken stickers, and so on), but different pages can have different stickers. Next, ask the children to make up stories to go with the pictures they just created with the stickers. Write it in the book for them. Give them guidance if they need it but be sure to provide only open-ended questions rather than write the stories for them. If a child gets stuck on a page that has four horse stickers, for example, you could ask, "What do horses do?" The child could say, "Four horses go for a run." Encourage them to connect the story from one page to the next rather than just make a statement on each page. For example, if the third page was "3 chickens in a barn," the next page could be "The chickens made so much noise that the 4 horses ran out of the barn!" Again, offer open-ended questions about how the pages can connect so the children come up with their own stories. Having number books with stories they personally created will make the numbers more personal and important to them. *This activity supports curiosity through the creation of story; creativity through stimulus freedom as children see that numbers have a place in story, not just on worksheets; and math development through a concrete representation of numbers.*

BIG, BIGGER, BIGGEST FIELD TRIP

Building stacks of blocks that are big, bigger, and biggest is fine, but showing children how this relates to the world they live in is even better. Take a field trip to a local apple orchard; it is filled with these opportunities. When you arrive, first ask the children to each make a fist and then to go into the orchard and find apples that are smaller than their fists. Next, they should find ones bigger than their fists, and finally, apples the same size as their fists. They will then have three apples they can line up—big, bigger, biggest. Next, take a walk through the trees and ask which they think is the smallest tree, the biggest, and in-between. How about branches? Leaves? There are many opportunities. Now go into the barn and ask to see the apple-sorting machine. Its job? To separate the apples into big, bigger, and biggest! Let them see how it's done and talk about why. To finish, buy some apples in various sizes to take home and sort. *Activity supports curiosity through exploration of our world, the possibilities through comparisons, and creativity through stimulus freedom as children not only begin to see their surrounding for what they are (an apple orchard) but learn to apply concepts to them as well. Activity also supports math development by building a better understanding of big, bigger, and biggest and a concrete understanding of comparisons.*

THE GROWING JAR

Get a large jar—quart size or much larger if you can. Have the children fill the jar with a variety of items, one type at a time. For example, have them fill the jar with toy cars and then dump out the cars and count how many fit. Next, have them fill it with pom-poms, and again, dump and count. Next, buttons. Next, beads. Draw a chart for the children to show how many of each of the items fit into the jar. Talk about how the jar did not grow but the number of items that fit into it did—why? After doing a few items, before filling the jar with a new item, have the children guess whether they think more or less will fit into the jar compared to the previous item. *Activity supports curiosity through exploration of items, comparisons of sizes, and experimentation while also supporting math development through counting and number comparison.*

COLOR FIELD TRIP

Teaching your children about colors? Let them know that colors are found all over in our world—especially in our food! Take a field trip to your local grocery store. Assign a color to each child (you can give them colored pieces of paper or draw squares of the colors with crayons or markers). Take your time walking down the aisles, finding foods of various colors. If the kids can't find certain colors, have them ask for help from the clerks. As they find foods, talk about whether these are healthy foods or treats—for example, are the colors natural or created with chemicals? This is a great opportunity to show children how to find natural, healthy foods to eat. Be sure to purchase food in a few of each of the colors you find. When you return home, you can put the foods out and have a tasting party—have the children talk about which color foods they liked best. *Activity supports curiosity through exploration of our world and the possibilities of color and where it exists in our world while supporting math development and building a concrete understanding of color recognition.*

SOCIAL AND EMOTIONAL DEVELOPMENT

YOU MAKE ME FEEL LIKE DANCING!

Provide the children a variety of musical instruments and props, such as scarves and streamers. Play music and ask them to choose an instrument or prop during the song. Ask them to use these to reflect how the music is making them feel. Have them put a name to the feeling and use the instrument or prop to act it out through music. After each song, play a very different song that represents a different feeling. Encourage the children to experiment with different instruments until they find the one that best helps them represent their feelings. Also, have them experiment with how they play the instruments or use the props. *Activity supports creativity as children explore music and instruments and the possibilities they hold for expressing emotion and producing music while supporting emotional development as children find new outlets to express emotion and learn to recognize emotion through the actions of others.*

PEOPLE WATCHING

This is best done on a field trip to a busy place, such as a city park, library, or mall but can be done in a front yard if you've got some traffic outside—on foot or in cars. Ask the children to sit down and pay close attention to the people they see pass by. Choose a person and have the children imagine the answers to questions asked of the person, such as What is your job? Are you married? Does your grandmother live far away? Do you have a pet? Can you fly a plane? Do you work in a circus or as a photographer? Can you touch your ears with your toes? Is your favorite color purple? Is your favorite food broccoli? As you ask these questions, make them sillier and sillier to encourage the children to use their imaginations to consider all the possibilities. Before long, they will be coming up with their own questions and scenarios. You can even ask a few of the people if they would please stop and answer a question or two—you may be very surprised at their answers! I once did this at a state park with my group and we ended up meeting two men who were furniture makers from Germany. When you return inside, spend some time having the children write a story about one of the people you saw.

Activity encourages curiosity as children begin to wonder more about the people around them and form the questions they need to find out about them while also supporting social development as children learn more about other people in our world.

AND INTRODUCING . . .

Take a familiar story, such as "Little Red Riding Hood." As you begin to read the story, add a child from your group. For example, "As Little Red Riding Hood walked through the forest, she met Jack, who was sitting by a creek." Then, ask the children to help you decide what Jack will do in the story and how that will change the outcome. At some point, you will most likely need to put down the book as it will completely change the story! Continue to tell the story with the children's help until you create a new ending. You can write down the new story and have the children draw new pictures to create a class book. Do this each day so each child gets an opportunity to be added to a story and change it. *Activity encourages curiosity as children consider how they can affect the outcome of a story and also supports creativity as children experience the stimulus freedom of being able to change a previously written story. Activity also supports social development as children begin to empathize with the characters, building a better understanding of the actions of others.*

WHAT IF KIDS RULED THE EARTH?

What a great idea! Enough with the grownups being in charge—help the kids live out every child's fantasy and consider what the world would be like if kids ruled the earth. Ask them questions, such as What would you change and what would you keep the same? Who would be in charge—a child or a group or no one? What type of laws would you like to see (ice cream for lunch?), and what would everyone be doing each day? Let their imaginations soar with the possibilities. Write them down and create a story based on their answers, or have them create a play to act it out for the parents. *Activity supports curiosity as children wonder about how they could change the world and consider all the possibilities for change while also supporting social development as children see themselves as part of a society with the power to effect change.*

FIELD TRIP TO STATE CAPITOL

Often, adults tell young children, "You could be president some day!" Help make this possibility more concrete by taking children to visit local political offices—a state capitol, a mayor's office, or another elected official's workplace. Give the children a chance to question the politicians about how they got there and what it is they do. Possibilities seem more reachable when children get a chance to meet the real people who have made it where the children have only dreamed of going. *Activity supports curiosity as children consider the possibilities for their future and make connections to the real world around them while supporting social development as they learn more about how our society works and their places in it.*

FIELD TRIP TO SEE COMMUNITY HELPERS

Same concept as above—take children out into their communities to see who the people are who help serve and protect them. Firefighters, police officers, nurses and doctors, ambulance drivers, postal workers, librarians, and so on. Make these professions concrete for children and help them build relationships with the people who do them. Children are much more likely to reach out to people in the community if they have had some previous contact with them. It is an opportunity to build familiarity so the children feel connected to their community and understand it is filled with people who can care for them. *Activity supports curiosity and social development as children learn who the people in their community are and begin to understand the possibilities for themselves as a member of a community.*

PLAY SCHOOL

Children love to have the opportunity to reverse roles, to be the adults and feel the power they associate with being adult. Give them opportunities to try on leadership roles for size. Set up a dramatic play area for an old-fashioned one-room schoolhouse, lining up a few desks (make them with boxes) and with a chalkboard up front. Let the children decide who should get to be the teacher first, and everyone else (including the actual teacher or parent) will be a student. Provide paper and pencils, books, and other appropriate props. During play, allow the "teacher" to call all the shots, as long as they are appropriate. Play along and encourage the other children to cooperate. Have several children take turns being the teacher. *Activity supports curiosity as children have the opportunity to get to know the world around them from a new point of view, exploring new options and questions they may have and gaining new understanding while also supporting social development through role playing.*

PLAY ZOO

Read the children the book *A Holiday for Mister Muster,* by Arnold Lobel (1963). If you can't find the book, the premise is that Mister Muster is a zookeeper and all his animals are sick. The veterinarian says they need fresh air and sunshine, so Mister Muster takes them to the beach for a day, packing dozens of sandwiches and gallons of lemonade! They have a great time, but before they go, the animals spot a carnival nearby and run off. Mister Muster tries to get them to come back, but they are having too much fun on the rides. Finally, he puts on a moustache disguise and turns the bus into a carnival ride, calling it "the most amazing ride in the world!" All the animals get on the bus for the amazing ride. He drives them through towns and the countryside, and they end up back at the zoo. The animals are angry until he removes his disguise. He promises they will take the ride often, and the animals are happy again.

Help the children set up to act out the story. Someone gets to be Mister Muster, and the other children play the animals. Pretend everyone is sick in cages at first. Choose someone to play the vet; that child can go on to play an animal. Then use a couch or line up some chairs for a bus. Pretend a blanket is at the beach and pretend to make lots of sandwiches and lemonade and eat and drink. Then the "animals" will hear the carnival and run off; they can pretend different chairs are different rides. Give Mister Muster some blankets and ribbons to decorate the bus with, a pipe cleaner moustache and a hat, and then continue the story to the end. Children love to try out the different roles and to pretend to be animals on rides or that are sick. The person playing Mister Muster also gets to experience how hard it can be to be responsible for a lot of animals (or children!). The children will get the giggles as they pretend to ride the bus through the bumpy countryside. And everyone gets hugs at the ending. *Activity supports curiosity as children explore their world through the eyes of animals and consider different points of view while also supporting emotional development as children learn to empathize with different characters as they role play.*

ROAMING REPORTERS

Help the children construct a list of questions that they can bring on any future field trip to ask a stranger they meet. First, let them brainstorm as many questions as they like, writing them all down. Then, ask them to narrow the list to the five most important things they would like to know about someone. Write this list down, laminate it, and hook it onto your field trip backpack. The next time you are on a field trip, choose someone to approach and ask if he or she would mind answering a few interview questions. Have the children use a handheld tape recorder to record both their questions and the answers. Back at home or school, play the recording and use the answers to help the children write something about the person they met. They can draw pictures to go with it and post it on a bulletin board to be shared with others. *Activity supports curiosity as children learn to be prepared with questions, to always be on the lookout for new people to meet, and to always be open to learning something new while also supporting social development by encouraging social interaction.*

THE PUPPET REPORTER

Find a fun puppet that the children would enjoy talking to. The parent or teacher uses the puppet to interview each child. Ask the child to come over to a couch or chair. The adult hides behind it and holds up the puppet to the back of the couch for the child to see and asks them questions. Go from serious to silly with the questions, such as What is your name? Do you like your name? What other name would you like to have? Would you want your name to be Spaghetti? Why not? How about Knee Cap? What if I wanted to call you Shoelace? What was your name again? It's too hard to remember; can I just call you Cucumber? What is so funny? Is your mother's name Seaweed? It's not?! How about Garage Door—I'll bet that's it! Take a simple question, and turn it silly and see what fun comments come from the children. *Activity supports curiosity as children experience a questioning period that goes outside of the normal realm. They consider the silly questions, and in the end learn something more about themselves, supporting emotional development in the process.*

COGNITIVE DEVELOPMENT

TOUCH MEMORY GAME

Place three or four objects in a cloth bag or pillowcase (something the children cannot see through). Use objects such as a toy car, a ball, a paper clip, and a pinecone—things that feel very different. Ask the child to feel the items inside the bag without looking in. Then remove one of the items without the child seeing which one it is. Ask the child to again feel the items and tell you which one is missing. *Activity supports curiosity through exploration with the sense of touch and exercises memory skills to support cognitive development.*

MYSTERY MADNESS

Create a mystery for your children to solve. It can be as simple as placing a chair on top of the table before they arrive or placing a large box filled with pillows in the backyard—anything out of the ordinary. Or remove something, such as the couch or table—or *all* of the toys! Get the kids' curiosity going and let them work to solve the mystery. It all begins with one simple question: Why? You'll have to figure out what you want for that answer and give them clues to get to it. For example, Why is there a chair on the table? To find the answer to this, they will need to ask other questions, such as How did it get there? Who put it there? When did it get put there? After talking it over and recalling it was not there the previous afternoon but appeared in the morning, they will realize it was probably put there the night before. Then they would need to find out who was in the room the night before and discover that you, your teen daughter, and the dog were there. Finally, they will need to know what each of you were doing and learn that your daughter was washing floors for you. This could lead to the conclusion that the chair is on the table because she put it up there while she washed the floor.

Allow children to do as much of the questioning as possible, providing prompts only when they are completely stuck. Even then, provide more questions—not answers—if possible. Teach children to slow down when asking questions, to understand how one can lead to another and to more detailed information. They will want to skip ahead to an answer, but a good detective always collects all the facts and clues first. *Activity supports curiosity as children view questions as a means to collect valuable information about their environment and the possibilities within while supporting cognitive development through problem solving.*

STORIES IN MOTION

The next time you read a story to the children, whenever there is an action word, act that word out! If it says *skip*, skip. If you read *hop*, hop. If you read *run*, run. Do this throughout the book. Later in the day, ask the children if they can tell you the story you had read. You'll be surprised how much easier it is for them to remember it when you act out the story—the action will give them additional sensory input, making it easier to remember the story. To take it a step further, ask the children to do the actions with you for even better memory retention. *Activity supports curiosity through story and sensory experience while supporting cognitive development through memory practice.*

FIELD TRIP TO CHILDREN'S MUSEUM

Most large cities have a children's museum, and even if it is a bit of a drive to get to, it is well worth it as a yearly field trip. These museums have the funds to create environments that are amazingly interactive and creative and that pique children's curiosity. For example, at the Madison Children's Museum, they have life-size ceramic cows that children can "milk," a crane the children can use to pick up large foam blocks and move around, a shadow room that freezes the children's shadows on the wall, and much more! Take full advantage of the activities offered by first calling the museum or visiting its Web site to see what the current theme is so you can do some prep work with the children. Read stories and do art activities connected to this theme before visiting. While there, see if there are any activities you can re-create. Because there are usually many ideas and themes going on at these museums, take note of which ones really pique your children's interest so when you go back to home or school, you can build off this interest and explore it even further through more activities, art, music, and books. *Activity supports curiosity as children explore their world through the many hands-on activities offered at a children's museum and take these interests back home to explore further while supporting cognitive development through the many problem-solving activities offered there and the new information gained.*

ALL TIED UP!

Before the children arrive, tie the end of a ball of yarn to a new toy or game for the children to find, hiding it under a piece of furniture or a blanket. Then unroll the yarn, winding it around items and furniture in the room, crisscrossing the room, going up and down, creating a spiderweb effect that spans the entire room. Continue until the ball of yarn is used, keeping the end accessible. When the children arrive, let them know they have a surprise, but they must first unravel the spiderweb. Give them the end and get them started, showing them how to gather up the yarn as they follow it. Then let them work on their own to get to the end, finding their surprise and then getting to play with the new toy or game. *Activity supports curiosity through exploration of the possibilities as they consider how to gather up the yarn and supports cognitive development through problem solving.*

EXPERIMENT TABLE

Set up a table just for experiments considering the possibilities of a certain substance. It could be liquid, such as milk, juice, or oil, or solid, such as flour, dirt, snow, or salt. Provide the children a container of the substance to be experimented on and other containers with things they can mix with it to see what happens. For example, if milk is the item, you can have a jar of vinegar, a jar of oil, a jar of water, a jar of cocoa, and a jar of crushed nuts. Provide lots of spoons. The child can spoon a bit of milk into each jar to stir in and see what happens. Try to provide things in the jars that will give them different results—a change in color, a mixture, a combination that doesn't mix but that makes the substance sink or float, and so on. *Activity supports curiosity as children consider the possibilities of many different items, experimentation as they search for the answers, and cognitive learning through problem solving.*

WHAT COMES NEXT?

Focus on logical consequences with the children. Set up a variety of activities where one action will lead to another and as the children participate, have them stop to consider what the outcome will be before moving on. For example, give them each a small bucket filled with Styrofoam packing peanuts. Tell them they are to hold the buckets in their hands, tight to their stomachs, and jump. Before they begin, ask them to consider what will happen. Then have them jump (peanuts will fall out). Stop and discuss what happened, why, and if they had guessed right. Another activity is to shovel the sand in your sandbox into the middle in one big pile, as high as you can. Then tell the children they are going to get to run up and over the pile a bunch of times. Before starting, ask them what they think will happen as they try to run up the sand (they will slip) and what will happen to the sand pile (it will get smaller).

Be sure to set up activities whose outcomes will be unknown or different each time. For example, what if everyone spins in circles—what will happen? Surprisingly, not everyone will get dizzy! The dancers in the group will know how to turn, keeping their eyes on one spot to keep from getting dizzy. Or what will happen if you take a bucketful of small feathers and throw them up into the air—where will they fall? The answer will depend on if you are inside or out and if there is a ceiling fan running on high or if it is a windy day. *Activity supports curiosity through the exploration of possibilities and relationships of items in our world and supports cognitive learning through problem solving and the understanding of natural consequences.*

SAME/DIFFERENT OBSERVATIONS

Provide the children a variety of items for observation. Find items that have things in common but have differences as well. Help the children create a list of similarities and differences. Give them, for example, an apple, a tomato, a ball, a doll, and a bowl. Similarities exist between some of the items but differences exist as well. The similarity for all of them? They can all be found in a house! Help children to think outside the obvious when observing items. For example, a similarity between a tomato and a bowl is that they are both smooth. A doll and a bowl are both plastic. The children will probably surprise you with what they observe. *Activity supports curiosity through exploration of items from the world around them, questioning the uses and attributes of them while supporting cognitive learning through comparisons and differences.*

LATE LAST NIGHT . . .

Encourage each child to share a story about something that happened the night before. Ask questions to help the child elaborate and encourage questions from the other children as well. Help the child fill in details by having him or her name people, smells, colors, timing, feelings, and so on. *Activity supports curiosity through story and supports cognitive learning through memory practice.*

REMEMBER YOUR SENSES

Take a moment with the children in a given situation, such as on a field trip or during outside play, to stop and consider all of their senses during that moment. What do they see—what colors and sizes? How does the ground they are on, or the items they are holding, feel? Can they taste anything? What does it smell like? What do they hear? Help children isolate each sense as they consider it by closing their eyes or being still. Later in the day, stop and ask them to recall the senses from that experience. *Activity supports curiosity though exploration of the world around them and supports cognitive development through sensory recognition and memory.*

HEALTH AND PHYSICAL DEVELOPMENT

WHAT'S THAT WORD?

Choose a word from a storybook that is repeated often and is easy enough for the children to learn. Write the word on a chalkboard or sheet of paper to spell it out and teach it to the children. Then, when you read the book, tell the children to pay close attention, watching for when the word appears. Point to each word you are reading as you read slowly. For big groups, a big book works best. For one-on-one reading, any book will work. Tell the children that when they see the word, they should yell the word as they jump up! As they get better at this activity, you can expand to two or more words, giving them a different physical activity for each word, such as jumping, clapping, or turning in a circle. *Activity keeps children curious as they wonder when the word will appear and promotes physical development through large motor activity as they jump and have fun.*

Activity alternative: Teach children to be curious about the five *W*s and how. Pick one of the questions, such as *where*, and tell them that each time you read something in a book that tells a *where*, they should jump up!

JUST ONE MORE

Provide children an assortment of building blocks and ask them to build a tower by placing one block on top of another. As they build, talk with them about how many blocks they think they can place on the tower before it falls. As it begins to get close, encourage them to stop and pause before placing the next block and ask themselves, "If I add one more block, will it fall?" Encourage their expectation and curiosity in finding the answer. Then celebrate when the answer is found. Repeat the activity using a different set of blocks, and ask the children to consider if the number of blocks will be the same or why it might change. *Activity supports curiosity as children consider the possibilities when a block is added and promotes physical development through block building and large motor activity.*

DON'T THROW THE BALL!

Have the children stand in a circle and pass a large ball, such as a beach ball or exercise ball, around the circle without using their hands. They can use their legs or support the ball between two of their bodies, heads, bottoms, and so on. Let the children come up with creative ideas and keep going around until lots of new ideas have been shared. *Activity supports curiosity as children consider the possibilities for ways to pass the ball and promotes physical development through large motor activity using their entire bodies.*

PRESENT UNWRAP

Collect a variety of boxes starting with a very tiny one so that each box can fit inside the next-bigger box. Wrap the smallest in birthday wrapping paper, put it inside the next-bigger box, and then wrap that box as well. Continue to put the wrapped boxes into next-bigger boxes and wrap again. Give the final large wrapped box to the children and let them unwrap it, asking them to wonder what may be inside and to give you their guesses. As each box unveils another box, ask the question again. Children love to unwrap presents, and when taped well, wrapped boxes make a great small motor activity that's loads of fun too! Add to it the wonder factor, and you've got the perfect activity for fun, developmental learning, and sparking their curiosity. For the final box, you can choose to put in small prizes, or when they say it is empty, answer, "No, it's not! It's got a great idea inside!" Hold it to your ear as if listening, and then announce a game or that everyone gets to go outside to play. *Activity supports curiosity through possibilities, delayed gratification, and exploration while supporting physical development through small motor activity.*

MAZES

Children love to run through mazes. Create them in an open yard area using raked leaves, ropes, or hoses. They can also be made by mowing the lawn into a maze or by using straw bales for something a bit more long lasting. Be sure to include lots of dead ends and have one entrance and one exit. In addition to having the children go start to finish through the maze, divide them into two groups—one at each opening, give a signal, and have both groups go into the maze and see where they meet up. That place will likely change each time they do it. *Activity meets the children's need for curiosity as they anticipate where each path will lead them, supports problem solving as they rule out the dead ends, and supports physical development through large motor activity as they run through the maze.*

SHOE KNOTS

Gather all the shoes of the children—yours too—and start tying the shoelaces from one shoe to another. Make regular knots with bows so they can be undone fairly easily. Don't do them in a string—mix it up! Make a real tangle of them. Then let the kids at them to get them untied. *Activity supports curiosity as children work to solve the problem of the tangle of knots and supports physical development through intense small motor activity.*

TO BE OR NOT TO BE . . . HEALTHY!

Make a list of healthy habits for the children, such as dressing appropriately for the weather, eating healthy foods, brushing teeth, washing hands, drinking water, exercising, and sleeping. Illustrate the list using pictures from magazines. Next, talk about the list with the children and ask them to consider what would happen if they didn't do these things. Go through the list one at a time and have them answer the question, encouraging some creativity by allowing them to act out the consequences as well. *Activity supports curiosity as children wonder something new and promotes healthy development as it brings a clearer understanding to healthy activities for the children.*

LET'S PLAY FIREFIGHTER

Set up a dramatic play situation for being firefighters. Find something to use as a fire truck—a couch, an overturned table, a lineup of chairs, and so on. Give the children a plate to hold for the steering wheel. If you don't have firefighter costumes, you can make simple ones by giving them red tee shirts or jackets, helmets of any kind (bike, motorcycle)—or make helmets out of ice-cream buckets. Collect vacuum cleaner hoses at garage sales (and from friends and family) to give them a truckful of hoses to use. A stepstool or other small "ladder" is fun to have as well as some walkie-talkies (or empty water bottles). Provide the props but let the children lead the play. Tell them where the fire is—you can even pretend to be a victim in the burning building. Allow them the opportunity to figure out on their own what they should do and how to do it. Taking on the role of the firefighter who tells the victims what to do to escape a fire teaches the children how they as victims should behave in a fire emergency. *Activity supports curiosity as children explore the world of firefighters and supports health as children consider how to stay safe in a fire.*

EXERCISE CLASS

If possible, invite an aerobics instructor to teach the children. If not, be the teacher yourself. Help the kids really get into it. If they have leotards at home, have them bring them to school, or they can bring other workout clothes (sweat suits, tee shirts, and shorts). Give the children water bottles and hand towels. Get some fun, upbeat music together. Lead them in an aerobics class, but let them help you come up with a routine. Stop often and ask, "What should we do next?" Start with stretching and a warm-up, and then do more active moves such as jumping jacks and lunges. Finish with more stretching and a cool down. Have them count the repetitions throughout. Keep it short the first time, maybe 10 to 15 minutes, but if you do it often, you can increase the length. *Activity supports curiosity as children consider possible moves for the workout and promotes health and physical development through exercise.*

THE ARTS

BUILDING THE "WRIGHT" WAY

Frank Lloyd Wright was an architect known for creating visually appealing and artistic designs that reflect nature. Encourage your young builders to go beyond the stack of blocks and other common building types to create a piece of art. Provide a wide variety of building materials and in the building area, for inspiration, post photos or posters of architecture that also represents art. Pique the children's curiosity regarding this art form.

Discuss architects and share their creations to help the children see how the lines of a building change the feel of the building. For example, Mr. Wright used only colors reflected in nature in his designs. The shapes also reflected the natural surroundings of the buildings, such as curves for a building near water and flat, straight lines for one on the edge of a rocky bluff. Art is a representation of the feelings and senses and can be done through many mediums, including blocks! *Activity supports curiosity as children consider the world around them and how it is portrayed by various artists while promoting the arts through architectural design.*

SOUND MATCH JARS

All sounds can be matched to a note on the musical scale by recognizing how high or low they are. Help children explore the range of sounds and find their matches by creating sound match jars. Collect plastic drink bottles and fill them with different objects, such as beads, small pinecones, rocks, and so on. Fill two bottles with each kind of object. Cover the bottles with either dark contact paper or paint so the items inside cannot be seen. The children shake the bottles to hear the sounds and can match them based on the sound they hear, comparing them as they go. For example, they shake one, then another. They hear the comparison—one sound is lower than the other—so they choose another bottle to compare. It is higher. They choose another, and those match. *Activity supports curiosity through sensory exploration and the arts through exploration of the range of sounds.*

A RAINBOW OF COLORS

Allow children to explore the mixing of paint colors. A large plastic plate or cookie sheet works well. The activity should focus on the creation of new colors, not a finished piece of art. It is a time for exploration, not production. Squirt a good-sized amount of red, blue, yellow, black, and white paint in separate areas on the plate or sheet. Give the children paintbrushes and encourage them to dip them in different colors and mix the paint together in a new place on the plate to see what colors they can create. Provide cups of water in case the children would like to clean their brushes between mixings. Help them name the colors they create and explore what happens when they mix two colors, then three, then four, and so on. When they have filled their plates with color circles, allow them to continue if they wish, blending together the individual mixes until the entire palette is blended. If at any point they wish to preserve what they've created, you can simply lay a sheet of white paper over the paint, rub softly, and pull up to make a transfer. Once the transfers are dry, the children can label them with the names of the colors. However, keep in mind the experience is to focus on experimentation with the colors, not to create a product. *Activity supports curiosity through experimentation with colors and promotes the arts by using paint as a medium for visual representation.*

MOBILE FUN

Help children explore balance by using a mobile to explore weight. Create a mobile using a long piece of string or rope and a stick, PVC pipe, or other sturdy, straight item. Cut each stick or pipe into three different lengths. At the end of the string, tie a loop in order to hang the mobile from a ceiling hook. At a height the children can reach, tie the string to the middle of the shortest stick. About six inches under that, tie the middle sized stick and six inches under that, tie the largest stick. On the ends of each stick, tie a six-inch piece of string. You may wish to secure all tied strings by wrapping a piece of masking tape or duct tape around the knot. Then collect miscellaneous items from around the room, being sure they can be tied easily—for example, a small ball is very difficult to keep a string tied around; a toy car would be easier. Start with the small items and ask the children to choose the two that they feel would weigh the same and therefore balance the first beam. Tie the two to the ends of the strings on the first stick, letting go to see if they balance. Allow the children to choose new items to experiment with until they find a balanced pair. Continue the activity using the other two sticks, using progressively larger items if possible until the mobile is full of items and balanced. Use the activity to foster conversation, asking questions about the items, estimates of their weights, and comparisons between the weights. With older children, you may wish to pair them and let each pair create their own mobile. By working in pairs or groups, the element of discussion remains and helps to focus the sense of curiosity and exploration. The result is not only a work of art but a lesson in math skills as well! *Activity supports curiosity through experimentation and supports the arts through structural representation.*

DIFFERENT ARTISTS, DIFFERENT TECHNIQUES

Collect a variety of posters of paintings by famous artists. Display them along a wall for the children to investigate. Encourage the children to look beyond *what* is painted to see *how* it was painted. What colors were used? Are the brushstrokes wide or narrow? Long or short? With soft edges or sharp edges? What else do they notice? Encourage them to get very close to see the small details in how the paint was used. Compare the paintings to each other—can they find a painting that has small brushstrokes and compare it to one that has large brushstrokes? How do they feel about the difference in how they look? How does it change the overall look of the paintings? Help children take the time to notice details in the paintings they may have missed at first glance. Ask them about how the different artists show light and depth and distance, looking closely to see the technique. Show children how, in places where it seems light is shining on something, that when they look closely, they can see it was done by using a light color such as white or yellow. Ask them which of the paintings they prefer and why. *Activity supports curiosity through exploration of the world around them and various art techniques as well as the arts as children learn about different artists, consider how art is a reflection of feelings, and how light and color can change art.*

Activity extender: Repeat the activity, only this time use a variety of paintings made by the children using different techniques and brush sizes. Ask the same questions as above.

HIT THAT NOTE!

Using a keyboard or piano, play a note for the children. Provide them with a glass (not a plastic cup), a metal spoon, and a small pitcher of water. Instruct them to fill the glass a little at a time with the water and tap it with the spoon to see if they can match the note you are playing. Help them explore with more or less water until they match the note. This activity can be done with one child, or for a group, have each child make a different note, and then line up the glasses to play a song on them! *Activity supports curiosity through exploration and comparison while supporting development of the arts through musical understanding.*

FIELD TRIP TO ART GALLERY

Visit a local art gallery, preferably one that has different forms of art, not just paintings. Help the children prepare by thinking of questions they may wish to ask the gallery director. Remind children to be respectful of the art they see and to keep their hands to themselves, and even in their pockets. Or better still, give them something to keep their hands busy, such as a pad of paper and a pencil. Take time to stop and let them draw pictures of the art they see. Choose a few items that you think you could try to re-create. Ask the director to explain how they were made and what materials you would need. Back at home or school, give the children the materials to re-create that style of art themselves (with their own artistic impressions, of course). Post the drawings they made at the gallery, and photos you take, on a bulletin board for the children and parents to look over and discuss. Display the re-created artwork near this display. *Activity supports curiosity as children explore their community and the types of art produced in their area as well as supports the arts as children consider new mediums to use to represent their ideas.*

HOW DID IT DO THAT?

Explore musical instruments with the children, helping them connect the actions and materials needed to produce specific sounds. For example, play music on the piano and then open the top so the children can see inside. Explain what the parts are and how they work. Play the song again while they watch the inside of the piano. For a guitar, violin, or other stringed instrument, play a song, and then cover the sound hole in the instrument with a piece of lightweight cardboard and play the song again. Discuss how it changed. For horns, after playing, place a sock or other item in the end and play again. If you don't have many instruments, take a field trip to a music store and ask an employee to help you do this exploration with the children. *Activity supports curiosity as children explore instruments and follow their natural curiosity in wondering where the sound comes from as well as supports the arts as it introduces children to a variety of musical instruments to play.*

WATER PAINTING

As opposed to "water paints," this activity is actually painting with water! This is best done on a warm, sunny day. Give the children cups of water and paintbrushes. Go outside to a sidewalk or driveway (any paved surface will do) and tell the children they can "paint" with their water on the sidewalk.

City Bound

Don't have woods nearby to explore? Have the parents bring the woods to you! Ask those who do have access to woods to bring in stumps and large branches to place in the playground for the children to climb on, explore, and build forts with.

Encourage them to do large paintings. As they paint, if it is warm, the water will dry up, and parts of the painting will disappear. When the children discover this, you can help them explore why it happened, letting them find the answers themselves. Make a game of having them try to paint their names quickly enough to get them done before any of it starts to fade away. While it may be sad to "lose" a painting, let them know that the good side is that if they make a mistake, they can wait a moment, it will disappear, and they can start again! *Activity supports curiosity as children experiment and explore how the sun affects their water paintings and supports the arts through their water expressions and techniques with brushes.*

Teaching Courtesy   7

Courtesy is a dying attribute in today's society. Evidence is that very few books even discuss it. With the exception of the books by Emily Post and by her daughter Peggy, I found very few resources on this topic. I also found it interesting that there was a time many years ago when these books were plentiful, yet over time the number diminished to the point of almost nonexistence. I believe we've seen a direct correlation to this in our society, specifically in our approach to teaching and caring for young children.

Sheryl Eberly (2001), author of *365 Manners Kids Should Know*, shares her concerns: "For at least a generation, manners training in many homes seems to have been neglected" (p. 2).

The negative outcome of this demise is we now have a generation of young adults who, while very competent on many learned subjects, have difficulty working in groups to accomplish tasks, have increasingly failed relationships and marriages, and have moving ahead in life as their ultimate goal.

In this quest for personal gain, courtesy is thought to be an obstacle, but in *The Modern Guide to Teaching Children Good Manners*, author Carol Wallace (1996) points out that "people with good manners are more likely to get what they want" (p. 1). Still, many people are cold and unfeeling toward others as they forge ahead to fulfill their personal needs at any cost.

But this cost is too high. Families are being torn apart by distance in our new world, and without some of the fundamental values encased in courtesy, they begin to see no reason to put effort into maintaining these relationships and often let them die. Businesses are floundering, with no sense among employees of responsibility as a group or from employers of loyalty to those who have served them for years.

Bringing a sense of responsibility and dependability between people begins with courtesy. Teaching our children to be kind and helpful to each other has a tremendous impact on society, yet it is missing in most curriculums in our nation.

Teaching courtesy has become such a novelty that you can even find one-week lesson plans on "good manners" or "friendship." The risk in creating these units is that teachers will see the topic as one to give their attention to for only a short time. Courtesy should be an integrated part of our everyday lives—in the way we teach, in the way we model relationships to each other, and in what we expect from children. Yet it has slipped away.

In the article "A Bat, a Snake, a Cockroach, and a Fuzzhead: Using Children's Literature to Teach About Positive Character Traits," Julia Kara-Soteriou and Heather Rose (2008) explain how they developed a unit using children's literature to teach about positive character traits. The authors say they decided to develop this unit "after Heather noticed how children in the class sometimes hurt each other's feelings when they thought they were being funny" (p. 31). The unit uses storybooks by Janell Cannon, such as *Stellaluna* and *Verdi*, to provide good role models for the children. They present this unit in the article, providing teachers a guide to teaching positive character traits to children. However, the authors concede at the article's end that "good character is not formed by the end of a short unit on good character traits; rather, good character develops over time" (p. 35). They see the unit as "a very good start." And they are correct on both accounts. Too often, teachers will produce a unit on manners, kindness, or positive character traits, and then put those ideas to the side. While it is very helpful to focus directly on the issue of courtesy for a unit, teachers and parents must remember that it is an ongoing learning objective that should remain an integrated part of their day.

Author of *Character Education* Sharron L. McElmeel (2002) agrees with the *Teaching the 3 Cs* approach to courtesy: "We must find ways to infuse our curricula with character building" (p. xix). As with our first two Cs, two ways to bring courtesy back into our classrooms and homes is for adults to model this behavior and to create environments for the children that encourages this behavior among themselves.

We discussed in the previous sections the importance of outdoor play for children. Richard Louv (2005) shows us the connection that outdoor experiences can have on a child's social skills: "Children who spend more time playing outdoors have more friends. Certainly the deepest friendships evolve out of shared experience, particularly in environments in which all the senses are enlivened" (p. 78).

By adding elements that engage children in exploration of the senses, we are providing them with a framework for discussion and cooperation. Children in environments that allow them to make their own choices, to create their own learning, will naturally work together to advance this type of play, fostering positive social interaction and lasting friendships.

Opportunity for positive social interactions paired with strong adult modeling is a recipe for success and an integral part of a movement to keep courtesy skills on the table. This movement is led by the Search Institute®, a nonprofit organization based in Minneapolis, Minnesota, that specializes in research on children and youth.

In 1989, the Search Institute began a study of 47,000 children (in Grades 6 through 12) and identified what they termed the 40 Developmental Assets® that children need in order to succeed. The study showed a list of attributes and experiences that indicate a child's likelihood to succeed later in life, or "resources upon which a child can draw again and again." Between 1989 and 1995, the Search Institute verified the importance of the asset framework, following 250,000 youth in 450 communities. The more assets a child had, the more unlikely the child would engage in problematic behavior, such as alcohol or drug use, sex, or violence, or have depression or problems in school (Benson, Galbraith, & Espeland, 1998).

Schools, community groups, and congregations around the country are seeing the value in these assets and participating in the Search Institute initiative to bring them into focus in their programs. In 2008, there were 600 initiatives in 44 states. The Search Institute initiatives span seven countries: the United States, Canada, United Kingdom, St. Lucia (West Indies), Australia, South Africa, and the Philippines (Benson et al., 1998).

The 40 Developmental Assets for early childhood are broken into two main categories: external and internal. Among the 20 assets categorized as internal, courtesy plays a major role. "Positive values" is an entire subsection of this category that addresses issues of courtesy, including these assets:

- Caring
- Equality and social justice
- Integrity
- Honesty

The Search Institute sees these assets as part of the overall framework that can identify a child's ability to grow, learn, and become a positive, contributing member of society. These are all assets embedded in our third C, courtesy.

In *Starting Out Right*, by Nancy Leffert, Peter L. Benson, and Jolene L. Roehlkepartain (1997), the authors state: "Early childhood experiences can provide a foundation for children to internalize these assets as they develop cognitive, moral, and social capacities" (p. 16). Much of the focus of the initiatives is to improve adult/child interactions, build strong role models, and create support systems for children. "The development of these values is a long process that entails many interactions between children and adults" (p. 65).

Teachers have long recognized the importance of these values but have felt constrained by the early learning standards adopted by their states. The 40 Assets Initiative affords them the opportunity to bring these values back into the classroom. Assets building is an approach, not a program. It provides a framework for action that encourages all individuals to make a difference. While this is good news for our elementary schools, these types of initiatives are a fairly new concept to early childhood programs.

A large proponent of the assets for all ages is the Young Men's Christian Association (YMCA). The nation's 2,686 YMCAs, serving 21 million children and adults, have created an alliance with the Search Institute and YMCA Canada, forming the Abundant Assets Alliance. The alliance partners have developed a holistic, systematic approach using the 40 Developmental Assets to improve the lives of young people by involving the entire community. YMCA of USA and YMCA Canada are implementing the approaches set out by the assets in all their staff training, programs, and outreach. The YMCA commitment to "build strong kids, strong families, strong communities" fits perfectly with the goals of the assets.

Emily Post said, "Learning manners builds character through the promotion of values including: consideration for the sensibilities of others, respect, honesty, self-control, trustworthiness, fairness and sportsmanship. These qualities enable men and women to face whatever the future may bring with strength, courage and integrity" (cited in Post, 2002, p. xiv).

The implementation of the 40 Assets Initiative is just one tool to bring opportunities for courtesy back to the classroom. But raising children who understand courtesy goes beyond basic kindness and caring about each other, according to the authors of *Starting Out Right*, who warn us that "the well-being of society rests on all people knowing how and when to suspend their own personal gain to help the welfare of others" (Leffert et al., 1997, p. 65). They stress how these values of courtesy (integrity, honesty, and responsibility) can increase the likelihood of school success for children but that they begin in early childhood by being exposed to adults modeling these values.

Deborah McNelis (personal communication, April 6, 2009), brain development expert, author, educator, and creator of "braininsights" materials points out that character education is essential in the early years: "A very critical time for emotional development to take place is from birth to 18 months. A child's brain makes connections based on the experiences in their environment. The experiences that are repeated often are the connections that become the strongest." She explains that once these foundations are created, the growth of a child who has received loving, caring interaction and the child who has not are very different. "A child that is exposed to lots of cuddles, laughter, smiles and positive caring language is going to have the caring systems in their brain activated and reinforced. Conversely, a child that is neglected or is living with many demands, commands, and stress is going to have the fight or flight response areas of their brain reinforced."

With these early brain connections being made so long before they reach us in an early childhood program, is it too late to change the child's outcome? Not at all. According to McNelis, "The good news is that repetition can change the brain, so early care settings can provide the positive experiences all children need. The child that has had positive experiences early is going to get the reinforcement to continue a healthy emotional development that will lead to the aspects of courtesy. For the child that did not have positive opportunities early in life, the daily repetition of positive caring interactions in an early care setting can make changes to the early brain wiring. It takes a lot of consistency but the earlier it occurs, the better chance for making a change."

Our role as models of courtesy and kindness is more important than ever. The children can't wait until grade school to experience character education—it needs to begin as early as possible.

What we expect from our children in regard to courtesy will depend on each child's developmental level. Manners expert Peggy Post (2002), daughter of Emily Post, stresses the importance of understanding our child's developmental capabilities and emotional needs, stating that this "helps parents to set realistic etiquette goals and expectations" (p. xiv).

Teaching children courtesy is best done as an integral part of their daily activities. Peggy Post (2002) tells us that "etiquette education is inseparable from the other things parents must do to rear responsible, self-sufficient adults" (p. xviii). She recommends beginning at birth, teaching infants by modeling basic values and behavior, helping them to build trusting relationships, seating infants at the family table, and establishing basic limits and routines.

As infants become toddlers, we build on this base by introducing sharing and cooperating, teaching them polite speech and basic rules of manners, such as at the table and in public.

By the preschool years, parents can begin to focus on helping their children develop values and empathy by introducing the concepts of honesty and respect, teaching good sportsmanship, and practicing greetings, introductions, and telephone manners.

Peggy Post (2002) says, "By integrating etiquette education into general development, treating the teaching of manners as a gradual and continuous process, and focusing on how well a particular child learns (rather than setting exact deadlines for learning), parents will find that teaching etiquette is not the struggle they may have anticipated. This developmental approach benefits children by encouraging parents to set reasonable goals and flexible limits" (p. xxii).

Teaching courtesy to children is a process of modeling and encouraging four elements that support this behavior:

- Dependability
- Kindness
- Honesty
- Respect

Teachers and parents can help children practice these values and provide a model for children to learn from. We've fallen into the bad habit of thinking these elements of courtesy are either not necessary or that someone else will teach them to our children.

This is not the way *we* were raised. Why are we raising our children this way? I ask every reader to spend a few moments thinking back to your own childhood. Do you remember just what *family* meant? Do you recall the prompts of courtesy from your mother—"What's the magic word?" Would you have ever considered lying, knowing the consequences would be severe? It's time to get back to teaching these basics, but in a better way, before they disappear altogether.

I'm going to share a lot with you in this chapter about my own family. These issues were central to how we were raised, and I believe they illustrate not only the importance but the outcome of including courtesy in everyday learning. No, we weren't perfect. My parents made mistakes, just as I do as a parent now. But courtesy involves people, and I think that sharing the stories of real people, rather than quoting statistics, can help you see the true impact of these concepts.

DEPENDABILITY

Children learn dependability by growing up surrounded by people they learn they can depend on. Of all the aspects of courtesy, this is the one that relies most heavily upon adult actions. More powerful than any activity you can create for the children, surrounding them with adults they can count on will embed in their lives the experiences that make dependability a part of who they are.

This is how I learned dependability. It began with my parents and extended to my aunts, uncles, and grandparents. Although I didn't realize it then, I see now how it affected us children: my sisters, my cousins, and me. When Dad asked us to do something, we did it. Not just because of the consequence of defiance, but because we respected him, loved him, and were eager to make him happy, to make him proud. And I realize now that because he had always been someone *we* could depend on, we wanted him to see he could depend on us too. I'm not saying we were perfect children—we had plenty of fights about who had to do the dishes! But somehow, we could distinguish between the everyday and the important, and we knew when it was time to step up to the plate.

I have over 100 first cousins. No, that's not a typo—I have over *one hundred* first cousins! Obviously, both my parents come from large families, and most of my aunts and uncles have large families as well. I couldn't tell you the names of each of them if my life depended on it. But if something happened that my life depended on, I know that each and every one of them would be there for me. In a heartbeat.

I've experienced this firsthand many times in my life, the most recent of which was in the summer of 2007. My dad (lovingly known as "Uncle Vern" to many, related or not) had been diagnosed with cancer. Lymphoma was quickly overtaking his brain, and we were told he had approximately two weeks to live. My dad was not scared by this. He had never taken life for granted and lived each day as if it were his last, so he had no regrets, no missed opportunities to grieve for. He insisted that he did not want what he called a "pity party" for a funeral, and that the idea of having hundreds of relatives show up when he was dead instead of realizing it was more important to see him while he was alive, really ticked him off. So we grabbed the phone and started to dial. In less than two weeks, we had over 300 relatives and friends come to the house to visit with Dad in his last days. He had hours and hours of conversations remembering good times, laughing, and simply embracing the gratitude of the moment and opportunity for one last hug.

I have a cousin who lives in California, is an extremely busy business-man, and hasn't come back to the Midwest in years. The day he got the call, he booked a flight and was at the house the next morning. He stayed by Dad's side for 24 hours and took the opportunity, as we all did, to extract what little more sound advice and rock-solid common sense Uncle Vern could give him, as he had for all of us, all our lives.

Growing up, every one of us had a time in our lives when we really needed someone, and Uncle Vern always stepped up to the plate. Because he had modeled dependability for each of us throughout our lives, there was no question that in turn he would be able to depend on us. From California to Florida and everywhere in-between, the relatives came streaming in. Laughter filled a home that was teetering on the brink of disaster. At Dad's funeral, we fulfilled our promise to him, gathering together once more, toasting one of the greatest men any of us ever knew, and then singing his favorite song: "Oh Lord, It's Hard to Be Humble." A huge joke in our family considering Dad could not have been more humble.

In my years doing child care, I often heard parents discuss difficulties in their own families. My heart simply broke for the children in my care who I knew would never have the kind of experience I had when my dad passed away. Often, parents become so busy that they feel they simply don't have time for these lessons, thinking that somehow their children will just know, just learn it on their own. But you can't learn about family, or being there for a friend, unless you are surrounded by them and they are there for you while you are growing up. A common phrase I heard growing up was "treat others how you want to be treated." I agree with this wholeheartedly. I believe we can teach others how to treat us through our own actions, and as adults making an impact in the daily lives of children, this should be a mainstay of our daily behavior.

In today's society, most children do not have dozens of aunts and uncles and over 100 first cousins that they can learn dependability from. Because of this decline in opportunities to foster dependability through relationships with extended family, a major portion of the Search Institute's 40 Assets is dedicated to ensuring each child has a support system—people to depend on. Older children have many opportunities for this as they join sports teams, clubs, and other groups. They build dependable relationships with coaches, teachers, team and religious leaders, and other group leaders. But in the early childhood years, finding these people can be a challenge. Young children are not typically involved in a wide variety of groups. Their relationships with adults are often limited to parents, their early childhood teachers and child care providers, and only possibly a few grandparents, aunts and uncles, or neighbors.

For this reason, it is more important than ever for early childhood teachers and parents to build relationships with children that they can trust and depend on. When a child needs you to help or to just listen for a while, it's important to take the time to give the child your full attention. It's not a numbers game. A child can learn dependability because one person—you—made the commitment to show that you can be depended on.

This is done over time and in many small ways. One example is when a parent arrives to pick up a son or daughter and asks the simple question,

"How did my child's day go?" A child who hears the teacher reply by reciting a list of the child's wrongdoings throughout the day will think, "You tattled." The child will lose trust in the teacher, feel betrayed, and no longer see that teacher as a friend, much less someone to depend on. Furthermore, there is a high likelihood that at the next pickup, the child will misbehave in an attempt to keep the teacher from talking with the parent and tattling again! Note that the same is true for parents when they drop off a child and spend this time sharing the child's wrongdoings from that morning or the night before.

While we may understand our role as educators and parents, we need to remember that in a child's eyes, we are also a *friend*. When we become a friend the child can depend on, we lay the brickwork on the road of dependability. So someday, when that child's "Uncle Vern" calls, the answer will be "I'll be there!"

KINDNESS

In addition to learning to count on others and become reliable, courtesy is about simple kindness. Doing things for others—not for personal gain but simply to make them happy. Again, this was something modeled for me in my family and a part of our everyday living. I have three younger sisters, and our memories of growing up together are filled with acts of kindness. Like when they let me play the role of "Mother" in our pretend play because they knew that role was my favorite. Or when Karen would take the time to braid our little sister's hair before school when she was student of the week, even though it meant not having time to do her own. Or when I took Jane out to the woods to build a fort when I was 15—I would rather have been hanging out with friends at the mall—because I realized that she was missing out on the things I did at her age simply because the rest of us had gotten too old for them. We thought about each other, empathized with each other, and did our best to bring some happiness into each others' day.

My mother was the one who showered us with kindness in the hopes we would spread it around among ourselves now and then. Our happiness was a central part of her life, and she spent much of her time doing for us all she could. Both she and Dad fully believed that actions spoke louder than words and that it was through actions that we could truly show others how much we cared.

Mom modeled this for us when talking about Dad and how she knew how much he loved her. One of the things we used to bug Dad about was that he would bring Mom a bouquet of flowers he had picked from a ditch, and we felt that if he really cared, he would have called a florist to have something nice delivered. Mom, however, would disagree and come to his defense. She explained that it didn't take much "action" to pick up a phone and order flowers, so it didn't mean a lot to her. Instead, Dad, who worked long, hard days in construction, would take the time on his way home to stop the truck, when he was tired and would just like to get home to rest, get out, walk around in a ditch to pull flowers until he had a nice bouquet, and climb back up to the truck to bring them home to her with a smile and a kiss. *This*, she told us, was an act of kindness. Even though it meant some sacrifice on his part, he did it in order to bring her some happiness. It wasn't the size of the bouquet that mattered; it was the size of the emotion behind it.

Alexis Shares Her Smile

Outside on the swings one day, Alexis was giving me the biggest smile, and I said, "Alexis, I love the smile that you brought to school today! Where did you get it?"

She answered, "At the store."

"Who bought it for you, Mommy?" I asked.

"No, Daddy bought it for me," she said.

"Well, I really like it. I think you should bring it to school every day," I said.

"Okay," she said. "I ask Daddy to buy more and I bring it to school every day."

"Do you think you could buy a whole bunch and keep them in your cubby?" I asked.

"Not in my cubby," she said. "I share them with Rochelle and Ethan!"

"Great idea!" I answered.

Recently, I was helping in a fourth-grade classroom when the teacher, Mrs. Sprecher, gave the children an activity in which they needed to work together to create something. She told the children, "Sometimes, it's okay to give in to other kids." She wanted them to consider the ideas of the others and not simply push to get their own ideas adopted by the entire group. In an age when children are typically taught to stand up for what they want, to go for their goals whatever the cost, or are raised by parents who give them anything they want, it was nice to see an educator teaching the value of kindness. Even when we really want something, to put the desires of another ahead of our own is an honorable act that can result in much more than what we originally wanted.

Acts of kindness can be spontaneous or planned. Each has the same effect—showing care and concern for another above your own needs and desires. Opportunities for this are abundant in an early childhood classroom. It can be as simple as suggesting that one child share a toy with another or something complex, such as a birthday party.

I had a family at my day care who had a newborn in the hospital for some time due to heart problems. So when the day came that four-year-old

Hannah announced her baby sister was coming home, we were very excited for her! I asked the other families to each make a casserole for the family but to keep it a surprise. The children became very excited about our "secret mission," helping their parents create the dishes. That week, on field trip day, the families brought their dishes. We loaded everything in the van and drove to Hannah's house to deliver the meals. Her parents were very surprised and touched by the visit, and the children felt such pride in helping them out. We also brought the "welcome home" cards each child had made. It was a special trip for everyone.

Taking the time to get to know families—their birthdays and big events, such as a new baby or a new house—provides teachers with many opportunities to teach kindness. Creating cards, making a special treat, or delivering meals or gifts all show the children good manners and the joy of an act of kindness.

Sheryl Eberly (2001), author of *365 Manners Kids Should Know*, tells us how teaching manners can actually help parents and teachers achieve goals of empathy and self-esteem for their children: "As they begin to understand the reciprocal nature of thoughtful conversation, they'll develop sensitivity toward others and be confident in new situations" (p. 74).

Another great place to begin these periods of "thoughtful conversation" is at the family dinner table. Sheryl says "the family table is a place of such importance—not only do children satisfy their hunger, they learn self-control, family values, conversation skills and how guests are welcomed" (p. 108).

In addition to traditional mealtimes, a wonderful activity that fosters polite conversation, good table manners, and basic kindness is the tea party. At my preschool, every Friday was Tea Party Day. We began each morning with a baking activity (great for creativity and curiosity). Then, late morning, we would get dressed up (I liked the purple feather boa), hats included, set the table (often outside) with a lace tablecloth and real china teacups and plates, and have a tea party. We ate whatever we had baked and drank tea sometimes, but more often it was milk or lemonade served in a real teapot the child of the week would choose from my collection.

This was such a special and fun time for all of us. It gave me an opportunity to model the behaviors I was working to teach them, and the children an opportunity to practice them in a fun way. We would ask each other about how our day had been or what we did over the weekend or what we looked forward to. Lots of pleases, thank-yous, and you're-welcomes, and compliments to the bakers for the delicious treats. I taught them how to properly hold a teacup and saucer and how to pour the tea, emphasizing gentle care of the special dishes. In 17 years, we never broke a cup. These times of special, kind, and courteous conversation and action became priceless memories for all of the children, and to this day, I get cards from past grads who mention them.

What a simple and easy way to begin—sitting down to a meal together and modeling kindness to the children we are sharing it with! Whether it's a parent who takes the time to write his child a note or a teacher who honors the ideas of her students, kindness is best taught through modeling. So what's your first act of kindness going to be? Got a child near you now? Give a hug!

HONESTY

Another core belief in our family was that lying was unacceptable. It was Dad's cardinal rule number one, and no one ever wanted to know what would happen if we broke it, so we didn't. We learned to face our consequences rather than seek to avoid them. The reason we could do this was simple: Dad made it okay to tell the truth.

The truth was so honored that as long as you were honest, no bad would befall you. No matter how awful the thing was that you did or how scary it would be to have to tell someone about it, you knew that by doing so, things would actually get better. Dad would tell us: "A mistake is a mistake only until you've learned from it. Then it's a lesson."

When we came to him and told him about our wrongdoing, such as breaking a window while playing ball, he would open with this line and then lead us through the lesson:

"What was the mistake?"

"What could you have done to avoid this mistake?"

"Is there a way for you to fix this mistake?"

"So what is the lesson you've learned?"

This process not only led us to be honest but taught us valuable problem-solving skills as well. It empowered us to face the difficulties in our lives rather than run from them. It made us strong. After going through the lesson, we would understand our abilities better and build our self-esteem because we understood that we were more capable than we had previously thought. By moving quickly from the negative (the mistake) into the positive (the lesson), we also learned the power of thinking positively and grew to be able to see the good in any of the bad we encountered in our lives.

When children are taught that they have the strength within to be honest, and that it's not about dwelling on the mistake but about moving forward to the lesson, they will be confident in their own abilities and learn to seek the positive in the negative.

Honesty is something we don't see a lot of in our adult world. Consider the profession of real estate. I would be willing to bet there are not many of you who feel there is a lot of honesty in the profession. Well, you've never met my sister Karen.

Karen is a real estate agent here in Wisconsin. She works part-time from home because her priority is being a wonderful mother to my two sweet nephews. 2008 was one of the worst ever for real estate agents. Over half the agents in her firm had to find other full-time jobs to make ends meet. My sister had her best year. Why? Because she's honest. We understood growing up that nothing good comes from being dishonest or deceitful—in the end, it won't be good. But when you are honest, things work out for the best. She practices this every day in her business. Most clients are a bit shocked at her honesty—but all of them appreciate it. She will tell clients when they ask to see houses out of their price range that they can't afford it and shouldn't stretch themselves so thin. She will tell them when the houses they are trying to sell are wrecks, and what they need to fix. She will refuse to take advantage of sellers by setting the price of their houses higher just to increase her commission. She gives her honest opinion about the houses her clients look at and the houses they are trying to sell. She gives real feedback, not a flowered-over version. She tells her clients honestly if she's done any work to sell their houses or not, and if she's got someone seriously interested or not. She doesn't lie to buyers about whether other people are looking at the house, and she doesn't promise to find houses for people looking. She never tries to talk someone into buying a house. She says that a house is a personal thing—it's a home, and it's either right or not and that the buyers will just know. Her job is to take them through houses till they find their home and tell her, not to try to talk them into something just so she gets a quick sell. Because of this, her phone has begun to ring a lot. Buyers and sellers who she worked with over the past 15 years are now calling her back again to help them to buy or sell once more. All of her closings are coming from repeat clients. They appreciate her honesty and integrity and become clients for life.

This is just one example of the power of learning honesty in childhood. I'm sure you can think of many more examples from your own family.

When honesty is supported in children's lives, it sticks with them. When they are met with negativity, they avoid honesty and lose it.

Children are naturally honest—it's not something we need to teach them. Rather, it is something to protect.

It's easy to be honest when there is no fear of a negative reaction. On a field trip once, an elderly woman came up to four-year-old Katie and said, "You look just precious!"

After the woman left, I asked Katie, "How did you get so precious?"

Her answer? "I just always be cute!" Pure honesty there—but easy. What about when it's hard?

One day, in the classroom of two-year-olds where I was a coteacher, the fire alarm went off. After emptying the room, we recognized immediately that John was not with us. I returned to the classroom and quickly found him hiding under a play structure—just below an open, broken, fire alarm pull. The director poked her head in my door to say no fire had been found. I replied that the alarm had been pulled in our room and there was no fire. She saw John too, nodded, and then left.

I sat down by John and said, "You look scared."

He nodded.

"Can you tell me what scared you?"

He quietly answered, "The alarm bell."

I said, "The alarm box is broken. When this breaks, the bell goes off. Did you know that?"

"No," he answered quietly.

"It would be scary to play with something and not know it would make an alarm go off. Did this happen to you?" I asked.

"Yes."

By my making it okay to tell the truth and not scary by approaching him with anger or yelling, he had risen to the occasion and remained truthful.

Honesty is often given little attention in classrooms today, and when it is, it is typically in the form of punishment for a lie. Teaching honesty isn't about what we *don't* want in behavior; it is about focusing on what we *do* want. It protects what the child instinctively knows how to do. When we bring this atmosphere of truthfulness into our homes and classrooms, we provide children with a safe place they know they can come to and honestly share their feelings and actions because they know that the importance is placed on their honesty, not their mistakes. Children treated in this manner will have a foundation for social interactions with adults that will also be based on honesty.

RESPECT

Everyone likes to talk about respect, but do we really practice it? Admittedly, it's a very difficult task. It means being able to show support for someone's opinion when it is different from our own. Sounds impossible. And it can be that way often. But it's something worth trying and striving for.

Teaching our children respect means more than just teaching them there are different opinions, feelings, practices, and cultures. It's teaching them to work toward a better understanding of these differences so they can come to appreciate them in some way. They may never *agree* with them or take on the particular belief or action, but they can at least make an effort to *understand why it's important to others*. To me, this is the definition of respect. Not just saying it's okay if someone has a different opinion but putting some action behind that and working to understand it better. It's not about saying we care about the issue; it's about saying we care about our friend who cares about the issue, and that makes it worthwhile to learn more about it.

Respect is more than showing care and understanding toward others; it also describes a type of

---

The Rock Star

Jack said to Hannah one day, "Hannah, a long time ago when I was grown up, I used to be a rock star!"

"Wow, Jack!" said Hannah. "Did everyone like you?"

Jack said, "They *loved* me! I was very famous. I went all over the world and everyone who saw me just *loved* me!"

"Wow, Jack, that would be great," said Hannah.

Jack said, "It was, Hannah. It really was."

---

honor that we place on others. To respect your parents or your boss is to honor their authority. It is often said that this type of respect is earned. This is true. It is earned when a person shows respect for others. A boss who is simply bossy and controlling is typically feared, not respected. A boss who works to understand his or her employees better and respect their strengths and weaknesses becomes respected.

When I was young, we kids were often asked to show respect for our elders. It is something that many older generations see lacking in younger people. We see the younger generation as having no respect—thinking they know it all and don't need our input in any way. Not appreciating someone for his or her knowledge or position is seen as a sign of disrespect. And it is.

But I believe we make a mistake when we simply demand that children respect adults they don't know. As I said in the beginning, the key to respect is in understanding. We need to respect our children enough to provide them the knowledge so they may come to understand the adults in their lives and the reasons why they should be respected.

"Understand the *why*" is a mantra I repeat often in my speaking engagements whether the topic is motivational, early childhood, or adoption because it opens the doors to so much. Especially respect. When we take the time to understand *why*, we build respect for each other. That shows us that we need to teach children to do the same. For example, as adults, we know the reason why a child should show respect for certain adults. You show respect for a teacher because she is there to care for you and help you learn and grow, and she has the knowledge to help you do this. You show respect for a guest speaker because he has worked hard to accomplish something (like writing a book or create a painting) and is willing to take the time to share it with you and help you learn more about it. But how often do we actually *tell* children these things?

I speak often at schools—with older children, to share my experiences of becoming a writer and with younger children, just to read them my children's book. I have seen the difference that the right introduction makes. If a teacher introduces me simply by stating my name and the topic I am to talk about and then reminds the class to be respectful, it typically fails. They are more apt not to focus on me and to continue to talk with each other until I've made some effort of my own to gain their attention and earn their respect. If, on the other hand, a teacher introduces me by explaining to the children that I have experience in writing that I would like to share and will answer their questions so they can learn more about becoming writers themselves, I have their full attention.

It comes down to something I use often in teaching any subject to a child: Connect it to them personally. If you want a child to understand anything from math to phonics to culture to respect, the most efficient route to that understanding is to make it important in their lives. How often do we remember asking our teachers when we were young, "*Why* do I need to know this?" Children today are no different. We've just gotten in the habit of not answering the question anymore.

If children grow up hearing the reasons why certain people need to be shown respect, they not only will be more open to showing respect for those people, along the way they will learn the qualifications that garner respect. Once they have a full understanding of what makes a person worthy of respect, they will be able to recognize it sooner and show respect more easily.

In *Don't Cheat the Children: Connecting Generations Through Grand Friendships*, author, educator, and intergenerational expert Helene Block Fields (2009) shares her research on intergenerational programs. In these programs, schools partner with nursing homes to connect children with older adults and create new relationships. She reports that when the children arrive at the nursing home each week, "it felt like a charge of electricity in the air" (p. 35). Children and adults alike would call out to each other with joy and admiration upon the children's arrival. Fields illustrates how intergenerational relationships are not only powerful for the older generation but of great benefit to the children as well, giving them wisdom, laughter, advice, and unconditional love. The children learn respect for the older generation by coming to understand them more fully during these relationships. Teachers and parents who encourage these "grand friendships" do much to teach their children respect for others. Fields's book provides many ideas on how to build a successful intergenerational program.

Respecting others—their opinions, their talents, their emotions—is built through empathy. As children understand others better, they build respect for them along the way. When they learn to put themselves in the other's position and understand it more fully, it becomes easier to see why this person deserves respect.

Web Sites for Courtesy Activities

www.character.org/

http://teachers.net/lessons/search.html (search for "character education")

www.braininsightsonline.com

Oprah is quoted as saying, "Leadership is about empathy. It is about having the ability to relate and to connect with people for the purpose of inspiring and empowering their lives" (Pink, 2006, p. 160).

Dramatic play situations are the perfect opportunity for children to practice respect, learn to empathize and work with others, and become leaders. In *The Creative Curriculum for Preschool*, authors Diane Trister Dodge, Laura J. Colker, and Cate Heroman (2002) state: "Research shows that children who engage in dramatic play tend to demonstrate more empathy toward others because they have tried out being someone else for awhile" (p. 271). This empathy leads to respect for others, so it becomes an important step in teaching respect.

As children create these dramatic play situations and learn more about each other, it also helps them to learn how best to interact. Dodge et al. (2002) tell us that "children learn to cooperate with one another by sharing and taking turns as they play a game or build an intricate design" (p. 295). The key to producing this level of cooperation is to have children negotiate their roles and agree on a topic. This means that children need the time, space, and opportunity to create their own play situations. As they learn to work together, they build empathy and respect for each other.

Part of building empathy for others is not only recognizing and respecting their feelings but having a solid foundation for understanding one's own feelings. When children recognize and name their own feelings, it helps them to be more open to recognizing and naming the feelings of others. Children often learn more about their own feelings through artistic expression. "Art is a natural vehicle for children to express their feelings. Children reflect their thoughts and emotions through their choices of color, texture, and media. Children also express their originality and individuality in their art" (Dodge et al., 2002, p. 317).

Artistic opportunities can help foster an atmosphere among children of respect, understanding, and empathy. As children learn to express their own emotions through art, they will better recognize the emotions of others in art.

Finally, books are a wonderful resource for teaching children empathy and respect for others. Through the story, children get to know the characters and can begin to understand their feelings and motives. They can explore outcomes based on emotions and how changing an emotion can change an outcome. They see the roles others play in society and friendships and learn from these interactions. They can see themselves in particular roles and build knowledge of how their actions affect others.

Children's Books That Promote Courtesy

The Children's Book of Virtues by William J. Bennett (editor) (1995). New York: Simon & Schuster.

Frog and Toad Are Friends by Arnold Lobel (1970). New York: HarperCollins.

Guess How Much I Love You by Sam McBratney (1994). Cambridge, MA: Candlewick Press.

Ladybug, Ladybug, Where Are You? by Cindy Szekeres (1991). Racine, WI: Western.

Winnie the Pooh by A. A. Milne (1926). New York: E. P. Dutton.

Providing children opportunities to build their sense of empathy leads them toward being more respectful of others. This respect creates a foundation for relationships, leading to dependability, honesty, and kindness.

Through an environment of honesty and support from the adults in their lives, opportunities for open-ended play, dramatic play, art, and reading, children will build a sense of who they are and who the people in their lives are and learn how courtesy plays a role in how the interactions between people will play out. When these children are also surrounded by adults who model courteous behavior, the lessons build more depth and meaning, bringing positive changes to their lives.

Courtesy Activities 8

In addition to modeling courteous behavior for children, teachers and parents can create activities and play situations that help foster courtesy among them. These activities all help to promote social and emotional development, included in most state standards. However, by focusing on dependability, kindness, respect, and honesty, activities that support social and emotional development can also bring courtesy back into the lives of children and build future leaders who are capable of empathizing and working with—and showing appreciation for—others while gaining reputations as people of honor and integrity.

DEPENDABILITY

PRINCESS IN A TOWER

In this game, the teacher plays a princess in a tower who is being guarded by an evil dragon. The "princess" can go to the top of a play structure or slide, and then the children need to find ways to save the princess. Choose a child to play the dragon. Each time you play, the children need to find a different way to save the princess. For example, feed the dragon so he's nice, use a magic cape to fly away with the princess, put a spell on the dragon, and so on. Each time you are saved, let them know you were not scared because you knew you could depend on them to save you! *Activity supports courtesy through active participation in behaving in a dependable manner.*

WHAT IF?

Play a what-if game with the children. Begin by asking a question about a social situation, such as What if someone is being a bully to your friend? What if you saw someone break a toy on purpose? What if you saw someone break a toy by accident? Leave it very open-ended, encouraging them to answer the questions without providing the answers or prompting them to reach conclusions you have preconceived. Let them use their own creativity to try to solve the problems. Simply acknowledge what is said during the discussion rather than use it as a springboard to give your own answer. Let children feel empowered by their own ideas! *Activity supports courtesy as children explore different social situations and the ways they can be dependable to their friends.*

HELPER CHART

Create a home–school connection by making a helper chart with four simple things that children can do at home to help care for their families, such as set the table, take out the trash, feed the cat, wash the dishes, or bring the laundry to the laundry room. Draw a square on the chart for each activity with either a simple picture or a name inside. Teachers can talk with children about the importance of being helpful to their families. Send the charts home, asking the parents to place a sticker over the square for any activity that has been completed. When all four squares have stickers, the child can bring the chart back to school for a prize, such as a new pencil. Use the finished charts (once all are returned) to discuss how it made them feel when they were helpful to their families and how it made their families feel. *Activity supports courtesy as children learn to be dependable members of their families.*

AMBULANCE DRAMATIC PLAY

Provide props for the children to play ambulance drivers, hospital workers, and those who need medical help. Use a couch or a line of chairs for the ambulance. Provide them with scrubs to wear (most hospitals will donate them to you), face masks, a toy doctor kit, clipboards, paper and pens, gauze, Ace bandages, Band-Aids, empty film canisters (for pretend medicine), a steering wheel for the ambulance and a big red cross for its side (made out of construction paper), and a stretcher (a plastic sled works well for this). Have the children work together to decide what roles each will play. Then let them go through the scenario of having someone get hurt, calling 9-1-1 (on a toy phone!), driving the ambulance to the victim, caring for the victim when the ambulance arrives, putting the victim on the stretcher, working together to get the victim into the ambulance, driving to the hospital, meeting doctors and nurses, carrying the stretcher into the hospital, and having doctors and nurses care for patient until he or she is all better. *Activity supports courtesy through role playing people we depend on in our society.*

TRAFFIC JAM

Using sidewalk chalk, outline streets to make a four-way intersection. Let the children ride bikes, scooters, or roller skates to go around the streets and choose someone to be the traffic cop. Provide the child a police officer's hat (police stations will often donate one if you ask) and whistle—even white gloves for more fun. Teach the "traffic cop" some hand signals for directing traffic and the "drivers" how to obey them. Then let everyone ride around and have the cop help to keep traffic moving smoothly in and out of the intersection. *Activity supports courtesy through role playing people we depend on in our society.*

WHAT I LIKE ABOUT YOU

At a mealtime, encourage children and adults to go around the table, turn left or right, and name the person sitting there as they finish this sentence: "What I like about _____ is . . ." It's nice to acknowledge something positive in friends at school and about family members at home. It helps build the self-esteem of those who are talked about, and the person giving the positive comments experiences how complimenting others can be rewarding. It reminds us that when we are not feeling good about ourselves or our day, we can always depend on our family and friends to see the good in us and lift us back up again. *Activity supports courtesy through experiencing the dependability of family.*

EVERY DAY IS OKAY

Talk with the children about things that happen every day that they can depend on, such as the sun rising and setting, their moms getting them breakfast, their sisters hogging the bathroom! Make a list on the chalkboard so they can see that there are many things we can depend on in our lives and ask about how knowing this makes them feel. *Activity supports courtesy by bringing a better understanding of dependability to children and connecting it to feelings.*

SUN, SUN, COME OUT AND GIVE US LIGHT

Read the book *How the Sun Was Brought Back to the Sky* by Mirra Ginsburg (1975). The story is about some little chicks who decide to go find the sun because it has been cloudy for many days. On their journey, they meet new friends who decide to come along to help them. In the end, they find the sun, who tells them he didn't think anyone wanted him anymore. They let him know how much they depend on him and help him clean up and shine again. After reading the story (or telling it), talk with the children about how they would feel if the sun did not come out for many days. What is it that they depend on the sun for? What would happen if the sun never came out again? What would they do—would they go look for it like the little chicks did? Talk about how we take things—even people—for granted sometimes and that we need to remember to show appreciation for the things we depend on. Finish by having the children make a picture for their parents to thank them for something the children depend on them for every day. *Activity supports courtesy through a better understanding of dependability as well as learning how to show appreciation for others.*

YOU CAN COUNT ON ME

Talk with the children about what others can count on *them* for. Who depends on them? What do others depend on them to do? Clean their rooms? Be good at school? Be good friends? Help with chores? Talk about how these people would feel if the child did not do the things the others depend on them to do. Ask if there is something new or different that others could start to depend on them for. *Activity supports courtesy through a personal understanding of being dependable and how it affects others.*

CATCH A FALLING FRIEND

This is an old standby trust activity that kids think is a blast. Have them choose partners and spend a minute talking with their partners about what they depend on the partners for, what they know they can count on from them. Then one child turns away from the other and says, "I'm depending on you to catch me!" and falls backward as the second child catches him or her. Encourage the children who were caught to hug their partners and thank them! Then have the children switch places and do it again. *Activity supports courtesy by engaging children in a situation where they will need to be dependable as well as depend on another.*

KINDNESS

CELEBRATE "ANY DAY"

Encourage children to show each other they care, that they are friends, by doing something special not just on a birthday or holiday but any day. Support them in giving spontaneous hugs and saying, "You're my friend!" Or have children draw pictures for each other. Encourage a child to go across the room to ask a friend to play or to share a toy. It's always a great day to be kind to a friend. *Activity supports courtesy as children learn to be spontaneous with acts of kindness.*

THE TEDDY BEAR SHAKE

Give children a fun and nonintimidating way to practice good manners when meeting people. Line up a row of teddy bears and ask the children to introduce themselves and shake their paws. You can pretend to be the voice of the bears or assign this role to some children. The kids will giggle and have fun but will also go through the actions and begin to view it as a little less scary than they originally thought. Give children the words to use: "Hello, Mr. Teddy. My name is Patty." And show them how to shake paws. *Activity supports courtesy through active participation in polite behavior.*

CAN SOMEONE GET THE PHONE PLEASE?

Have the children practice answering a toy phone. Model for them by picking up the phone and saying, "Hello, this is Patty" or something similar and short. Also have them practice how to make a call to someone else—"Hello, this is Patty. May I please speak to Jane?" You can use two play phones and have the children pretend they are calling each other. Role playing and modeling polite behavior helps children understand it better and remember it. To enhance their understanding, role-play answering the phone without being polite—pick it up and say, "Yeah, what do you want?" Then ask the children how that makes them feel. Talk about how the words and tone of voice we use on the phone show people respect and kindness. *Activity supports courtesy through active participation in polite phone skills and consideration of feelings.*

I KNOW SOMEONE WHO . . . GAME

Teach the children to share compliments with this game. Start by making a compliment about someone in the group, leaving out the child's name. For example, "I know someone who wears very pretty dresses." The children try to guess who you are giving the compliment to. The first child to guess correctly then gets to give the next compliment, choosing a different child to compliment, again leaving out the name. The game continues until everyone has been complimented. *Activity supports courtesy as children spend time reflecting on compliments about their friends and experience how it feels when others are kind.*

PLEASE AND THANK YOU

"Please" and "thank you" are standards of basic courtesy toward others. Model for the children how to use them correctly and prompt them when they can be used, praising the children when they do so correctly. The combination of model, prompt, and praise will help to make these skills second nature to children. *Activity supports courtesy as children learn polite language through adult modeling.*

SAYING "I'M SORRY"

Talk with the children about a time when you needed to apologize to someone. Let them know that everyone makes mistakes and feels bad about behavior choices sometimes, but these mistakes can be mended between friends by a sincere apology. Give examples of sincere and insincere apologies, showing the children that a thoughtless "I'm sorry" doesn't fix a situation as a true one does. By sharing stories of times you said "I'm sorry" and how you did it, children will see it as a part of relationship building and not as a quick fix for a mistake. *Activity supports courtesy as children gain a better understanding of other's feelings and the power of an apology.*

JUST BECAUSE

Teach children the joy of doing kind deeds "just because." Bake cookies together and take a basket of them to a local nursing home. You can also have the children sing some of their favorite songs for the residents while there. Encourage the children to ask questions of the people they meet. Before going, discuss what types of questions they may wish to ask. Take photos of the children with the residents and record their names so later you can label the photos and share stories of the people they met and what they learned. *Activity supports courtesy as children see the value in random acts of kindness.*

MAY I TAKE YOUR ORDER, PLEASE?

Role playing is great for practicing good restaurant manners. Children can practice sitting at a table, ordering politely, saying "please" and "thank you," using their napkins, and so on. Let them take turns being the waitperson and the customer. Give them props to add to the fun. *Activity supports courtesy as children actively participate in restaurant manners through role playing.*

THANK YOU!

After a guided field trip or speaker visit, help the children create a thank-you card. Let each child add something to it—perhaps a drawing of the child with the guide or speaker, a simple written "thank you," or something the child tells you he or she learned from the visit, which you can write. Let the children decorate the card and envelope with stickers or drawings. Mail the card or deliver it if you are able. *Activity supports courtesy as children participate in proper ways of showing gratitude.*

SETTING THE TABLE

Create a placemat out of construction paper on which you have traced all the parts of a table setting in their proper places. Let the children set the table for the next meal using the placemat as a guide. You can create a game of it as well, seeing how fast the children can set the full table properly or testing them by having them set the table without looking at the placemat and then checking to see if they got it right. *Activity supports courtesy as children practice table-setting skills.*

HONESTY

THERE GOES THE RIVER!

When children make a mistake or a mess, they learn to lie about it if they are always met with an angry response from an adult. They'll do anything to avoid this reaction. But when children are met with a positive response that encourages them to learn from their mistake and grow, they will lose this fear and be more honest about their actions. Next time someone spills milk at the table, instead of getting upset, call out, "There goes the river!" Calmly get a paper towel, hand it to the child, and ask where she thinks the river is headed. Is there any way to stop the river? Can she do it? When she does by putting the paper towel in front of it, have all the children cheer for her because she found a way to stop the river! Then have a conversation about how the river got started and help the children brainstorm about how to prevent another flood. Empower them to find answers, not lies. *Activity supports courtesy through action that empowers children to be truthful and to see mistakes only as something to learn from rather than as things that will upset others.*

CHORES ARE NOT MY SPECIALTY

Ask the children to think about the chores that they are *not* good at doing. Can they wash windows, scrub a floor, fold laundry? How about trim the trees, put wood in the woodstove, or mend clothes? Encourage children to admit where their limits are, letting them know that it's important to be truthful about what you can and cannot do. They should not promise to do things that are hard for them to do. Also, that not everyone can do everything well—it's okay not to be good at everything! Admitting what we can't do well encourages people to trust us when we share what we *can* do well. *Activity supports courtesy as children explore the truths of their limits and learn there is no shame in admitting they can't do something—being honest about it is more important.*

TIME TRAVEL

Ask the children to pretend with you that you are going into a time travel machine. Provide props, such as helmets and a big box to crawl into. Once inside, ask the children to think of something that they did that was maybe not so great and that they wish they could go back in time and change, such as forgetting to pick up their dirty clothes for Mom, taking out the trash for Dad, or not sharing a toy when someone asked. One by one, after they share what they want to change, pretend to push buttons to reset the time and travel back there. Then role-play with the child to go through the situation again and do it differently. Once done, get back into the time machine and it will be another child's turn. *Activity supports courtesy through a thoughtful examination of mistakes and ways to fix them, encouraging children to be truthful because they can always correct mistakes or do better next time.*

TRUE/FALSE GUESSING GAME

Tell the children you are going to say three things about yourself. One will be a lie and two will be truthful. You want them to guess which one is the lie. For example, mine could be "I have a cat. I have danced on national television. I have climbed a mountain." For me, the lie was that I have a cat. I once danced on "Club Dance," filmed in Nashville, Tennessee, and I went mountain climbing in Colorado on my honeymoon. Giving them a very believable statement for the lie allows me to talk with the children about how lies can often seem like the truth, that the children won't always know when someone is lying. But it's important for them to always be truthful so that others can depend on what they say. After giving your example, let each child give three statements (help them if necessary) and have the other children guess which is the lie. *Activity supports courtesy as children learn to distinguish between lies and truth while also learning that sometimes it is not possible. Therefore, they should always be truthful so that people will not wonder if what they said is a lie.*

TRUST CAN BE TORN AWAY

Cut a very large heart out of construction paper. Draw some sections on it (in a pie shape, so each is accessible from the outside edge) and in each section, write a task that children do that makes them trustworthy, such as clean their rooms, help with dishes, listen to Mom and Dad, keep promises, return something they find that is not theirs, tell the truth, play fair, and keep their friend's secrets. Talk about how when you tell someone you are going to do these things, you need to be honest about whether you can. Then give them an example of not being trustworthy, such as telling Mom you would do the dishes but watching TV instead. Then tear that section from the heart. Talk about how when the children are not honest or trustworthy, it breaks a person's trust in them. Give more examples for each section, and then tear out that section. Finally, with one section left, talk about how if you do these types of things over and over, after a while, there is no trust left in someone's heart and they will stop depending on you.

Then discuss ways children can rebuild the trust, reconstructing the heart using tape. Finally, talk about how even though they put back all the pieces of the heart, because it is held together with the tape, it is not as strong as it was in the beginning. Breaking someone's trust causes a lot of damage. You can rebuild it, but even then it sometimes isn't as strong as it used to be. The best thing is not to break this trust in the first place but to always be honest and trustworthy. *Activity supports courtesy through a visual representation of the cause and effect of honesty and trustworthiness.*

SIMON SAYS THE TRUTH

This is a variation of Simon says. "Simon" will say something he will do and then do either that or something else. If he tells the truth and does what he says he will do, the children are to do it too. But if he doesn't tell the truth and does something else, the children are not to follow him. For example, Simon says he will raise his hand. Simon raises his hand; the children follow suit. Then Simon says he will stomp his foot, but instead Simon claps his hands. The children stay still. When the children understand how it works, let them take turns being Simon. *Activity supports courtesy by engaging children in recognizing the truth.*

BOY WHO CRIED WOLF

This classic fable illustrates how sometimes a child tells a lie but sees it only as tricky or funny, but how others who believe it feel betrayed and after time, lose their trust in the child. After reading the story or telling it, help the children to role-play the story. Let children choose from the roles of sheep, wolf, boy, and villagers. After the children act out the story, stop and talk about how they felt about their parts. *Activity supports courtesy through role playing honesty and the effects of others on being truthful.*

RESPECT

SHOW AND LET YOUR FRIEND TELL

Hold a typical show-and-tell at group time, each child sharing an item from home and telling the other children about it. Then have the children give their items to the children on their right. Now each person stands up with the item and says why that item is important to the other child. This encourages children to take the time to respect their friends and why some things are so important to them. *Activity supports courtesy as children learn how to understand what is important to a friend in order to show respect to that friend.*

TRUE EMOTION GREETING CARDS

Help the children create a set of greeting cards that help them to show how they feel. In taking the time to think about how they feel, they will also have a better idea of how a person receiving a card feels. For example, if they know children who are sick, ask them how they feel about that. On blank cards (simply fold sheets of white paper in half), let them draw a picture that shows how they feel, such as of them playing alone, sad that the sick friend cannot play. Adults can help them put these feelings into words on the cards, such as "I miss you" or "Wish you were here to play." These simple, often-repeated sentiments will hold much more value to children who have taken the time to explore their feelings and come to these conclusions on their own. They can also take time to think about how their friend must feel at this time and instead draw a picture reflecting their friend's feelings. *Activity supports courtesy as children consider the feelings of others in order to be respectful when writing to them.*

WHAT DO YOU SEE?

This activity can be done outside or inside, at home or school or on a field trip—anywhere you want to encourage the children to explore and observe. Have them work in pairs. Ask them to explore the area you are in and take time to notice the details. To support this, you may want to provide them with magnifying glasses. As they find things, ask them to report them to you. Keep a list of each pair's observations for them on separate sheets of paper. After a designated amount of time (five to fifteen minutes is best), or when you return home or to school, bring the group together and hang up the pairs' lists in front of them. Read over them and talk about what is the same and what is different between the lists. Commend the children for noticing so many different things! Talk about how each pair noticed different items and have them talk about why they think this happened—we were in the same space, so why are the lists different? Help them to respect that their friends saw things differently than they did or thought different items were more important or interesting. *Activity teaches respect for others' opinions and observations while also supporting curiosity.*

I FEEL LIKE THE HUNGRY CATERPILLAR!

Choose a storybook well known to the children and ask each to pick a character from the story, pretending to be that character as you read the book. You can even insert the child's name in place of the character's name as you read. Ask the children to think about how their characters feel throughout the book. Take time to stop during the story and ask them what they are feeling. If multiple children have chosen the same character, have them share how they feel and compare to see if they share the same feelings or different ones. *Activity supports courtesy as children consider the feelings of others in order to gain respect for their actions.*

PLEASE PASS THE MIKE

Next mealtime, hand one child a microphone (either make one with a cardboard tube or use a toy one). Explain to the group that the person holding the mike will get to talk, and everyone else needs to be quiet and listen to what he or she has to say. Explain that when they are respectful and listen to their friend, they then earn the right to be heard as well. To keep it moving, give them an example of what to say, such as "My favorite thing I did today was _____." Encourage the child speaking to say "thank you" to the other children for listening before passing on the mike. *Activity supports courtesy as children learn to be respectful of others who are talking.*

WHAT'S YOUR FAVORITE?

Create a set of cards with questions about favorite things, such as: What is your favorite color? Game? Food? Pet, sport, song, art activity, bedtime story, place to visit?

At group time, read a card and have each child answer. Compare answers. To extend this to a math activity, create a graph of the answers to see which one was given the most. *Activity supports courtesy as children learn about differences and similarities in people and work to show respect for them.*

WATCH THAT TONE!

Teach children how tone of voice can portray how they feel toward someone. Let them use a tape recorder and practice making statements in different tones of voice, and then play it back and discuss how different each one made them feel. For example, "I would like to go biking" can be said with a biting tone, emphasizing the *I* as if angry and arguing with a parent about what different siblings want to do. Or it could be said sarcastically, emphasizing the *like* as if talking with disrespect to someone. Or it could be said in a sweet, kind, excited voice with the emphasis on *biking*, simply portraying happiness at being asked an opinion. You can model these types and then let the children come up with their own. Provide them example sentences to use in different ways, and be sure to discuss how they would feel if someone talked to them with that particular tone. *Activity supports courtesy as children build an understanding of how tone of voice can influence the level of respect they are showing as they speak.*

PLEASED TO MEET YOU, KING

Practice introductions by role playing with the children in fun roles, such as a princess meeting a prince, a movie star meeting an astronaut, the president meeting a queen, and so on. Let the children introduce themselves to each other in their roles and continue the conversation by asking at least one question of the other child. *Activity supports courtesy as children practice in a fun way how to be respectful with introductions.*

THAT'S SO-O-O-O-O FUNNY!

Talk with the children about the appropriateness of humor—when it can be truly funny and when it can sometimes be hurtful. Give them several scenarios and ask them to identify which is which. Read jokes from a joke book and talk about why they are funny, and then share things children sometimes say to other children to be funny but that can be hurtful. Talk about the differences. *Activity supports courtesy as children learn to be respectful of others and take time to consider what is funny and what is hurtful.*

BE PREPARED

Before taking a field trip or having a guest speaker, help the children show respect for the new people they meet by learning background information and preparing questions. Help each child come up with at least one question. Talk with the children about how asking questions is a sign of interest and respect for the person who is taking time to share something with them. *Activity supports courtesy by teaching the children to respect others through showing interest in what the children can learn from them.*

THANK YOU, YOU'VE BEEN A GREAT AUDIENCE!

Teach the children how to show respect during a performance by having several children perform as they wish on a stage and having the others, along with some stuffed animals and dolls, sit in rows of chairs as the audience. Sit quietly during the performance and clap to show appreciation when it ends. *Activity supports courtesy as children practice polite behavior during a performance.*

PHONE GAME

Use this classic game to illustrate the importance of good listening skills. Sit with the children in a circle. Whisper a short story to the child next to you. Ask the child to then whisper it to the next child. Continue to pass the story around the circle. When the last child has heard it, have the child tell the group what he or she heard. More than likely the story will have changed. Share your original story. Talk about how easy it is to miss important details when not listening closely and how easily untrue information can be passed on to others. Do the activity again to see if they can get closer to the original. *Activity supports courtesy as children see the results of gossiping and spreading stories and practice good listening skills.*

DRAMATIC PLAY

All types of dramatic play support learning respect by giving children the opportunity to take on the roles of others and understand them better. Dramatic play should be offered on a daily basis and for free exploration. To allow the children the maximum social benefits from such play, encourage them to cooperate when choosing their roles and their play's theme. Offer a set and props that lend themselves to a variety of play situations rather than setting up a dramatic play area specific to a certain type of play, such as a doctor's office. *Activity supports courtesy as children role-play and learn respect for others' jobs and situations.*

NEW NEIGHBORHOOD BUILDING

Give each child a small cardboard box to decorate. First, cover the box with construction paper to provide a blank slate to start with. The children should then decorate their boxes to make houses—not identical to the ones where they now live but unique to them. If their houses could look like anything, what would they build? Give prompts to get them started, such as Where else could you put the door? Would you have windows? What shape would they be if not square? Help guide the children with questions to get them to be creative with the outcomes. You can choose to have them draw their houses on the box or use collage materials to create it. When everyone is finished, using a large sheet of butcher paper or other roll paper, draw a street for them to place their houses on. Have the children add drawings or collage material to the street and yards to complete the project. Hold discussions about the new neighborhood you just built. What is unique about each house? What is similar? What makes it a neighborhood? Build the children's sense of respect for the work of others and that it takes many different parts to create the whole. *Activity supports courtesy as children practice respect for others' ideas and their contributions to large projects. This activity also supports creativity through stimulus freedom.*

Integrating Courtesy Activities

9

Most state early learning standards include content geared toward social and emotional development, which will include aspects of courtesy, such as empathy, cooperation, and respect. The following activities will help you ensure that the other skills inherent in courtesy will also become part of your program as you strive to meet the remaining areas of development.

LANGUAGE AND LITERACY

HOW DO YOU SEE THE STORY?

Talk with the children about how each person imagines a story differently. Illustrate it in two ways. First read a story that's new to the children without showing them the pictures. Then ask each child to share what he or she thinks it would look like—the characters and how they looked and dressed, the setting, the colors, and so on. Next, find several books of the same story, but done by different illustrators. Fairy tales and nursery rhymes, such as "The Three Little Pigs," "Cinderella," or "Mary Had a Little Lamb," are fairly easy to find several versions of. Show the books to the children. Read each of them. Then open the books to pages where the words are the same and compare the pictures that each artist drew. Talk about how the artists, just like the children, saw the story a little differently in their imaginations, so the drawings will be different—and each is okay. Get the children to really look at the details—the colors, whether it is a pencil drawing or ink or paint, how the eyes of the characters are done, the hands, the clothes, and the scenery. *Activity encourages curiosity about differences and details as well as builds respect for the opinions of others while exploring the creative side of literacy and how story can change based on the author's or illustrator's perception.*

WHY DID HE DO THAT?

Use a storybook as a springboard for discussions that teach empathy. As a character completes an action or shows a feeling in the story, stop to ask the children why they think the character did what he or she did or how they think the character feels at that point in the story. Get them to dig deeper by asking what could change in the story to make the character feel or act differently. The further the children explore a character's motives and feelings, the more they will understand and empathize with the character. Connect this to their real lives by asking if they have ever felt the way the character does or if they have a friend who has felt that way. This leads into asking what they think they could do if a friend felt that way to change the way the friend felt. Starting with a fantasy—the storybook—then linking it to their real lives is a great way to provide a model for the children and help guide them in their own friendships. *Activity supports courtesy through an exploration of other's feelings, building empathy and respect for others while building an understanding of story structure.*

Activity extender: To further a child's exploration of another's feelings and actions, ask the children what they would say if they could talk to the character. If that character came for a visit today, what would you ask him or her? How do you think the character would answer? If the author and the illustrator came, what would you ask them? *The activity extender also supports curiosity, encouraging children to look beyond their boundaries to the outer limits of their exploration possibilities.*

HANDS DOWN THE BEST FRIENDS EVER BOOK

Create a friendship book with the children by having each child make a handprint for everyone in the group, using paint on construction paper and with their fingers facing downward. Have the children write their names at the bottom. When dry, have the children pass out a copy of their handprints to each of their friends, keeping one for themselves. For each child, put all the pages together with the owner's print on the top. Write "Hands Down the Best Friends Ever" on the cover. Bind together by either stapling and covering the staples with masking tape or duct tape or by punching a series of holes along the binding edge and lacing together with brightly colored yarn. *Activity supports courtesy through the building of a visual that shows children in a storybook format all of the friends that they have that they can depend on.*

FRIEND POEM

Help children create friend poems, individually or as a group. For each letter in the word *friend*, create a sentence about friendship or a particular friend whose name begins with that letter. It can be a single word, such as *forever*, or a sentence, such as "fun to be with." *Activity helps children explore the meaning of friendship while supporting literacy as they learn to create poetry.*

BOOK OF VIRTUES

Read *The Children's Book of Virtues*, edited by William J. Bennett (1995), to the children. This book is filled with old tales, fables, and poems of honesty, friendship, dependability, and more. Encourage discussion after each reading. Also discuss the possibilities of the story's being real or fantasy. Talk about how it could happen if it were real. For example, "The Honest Woodsman" tells a story of a woodsman who finds axes made of wood, gold, and silver. When asked by a lake fairy if the axes are really his, he is honest and says they are not. In the end, the fairy rewards him by giving him all three axes. Talk with the children about being honest and telling the truth if someone asks if something is theirs or if they are able to do something. In the end, their honesty is always rewarded. *Activity supports courtesy through discussion of character-development behaviors and connecting the fantasy to reality while exploring literacy and stories of the past.*

PLEASE SAY PLEASE!

Another great book for discussion and fun is *Please Say Please! Penguin's Guide to Manners*, by Margery Cuyler (2004). Penguin has a dinner party with his friends, and each friend exhibits some bad behavior but learns the appropriate behavior. It's got great repetition that gets the children involved as they pick it up and help to repeat it during each scene. The book allows the readers to think about each action, decide whether it is correct, and suggest a more appropriate action. Great for lots of discussion and giggles! *Activity supports courtesy as children learn appropriate manners for a dinner party with a sense of fun and are able to become involved in the literary experience.*

FOX MAKES FRIENDS

This book leads not only to good discussions of friendship but to an art activity as well. *Fox Makes Friends*, by Adam Relf (2005), is a wonderful story about a little fox who goes looking for a friend. He decides to build one using natural materials such as apples, sticks, and nuts. When he has trouble building one, other little animals show up one at a time to help him. In the end, he is disappointed he was unable to build a friend until his mother points to the animals helping him and shows him that he actually had made many new friends. After reading the story, talk with the children about the different ways that they go about making friends. Then provide materials for them each to "make" a friend: apples, pumpkins, sticks, nuts, berries, pinecones, flowers, and any other item from nature. *Activity supports courtesy as children learn about building friendships and explore a story as well as leading to an artistic experience.*

THANK-YOU CARDS

Help the children create a set of thank-you cards that can be used after speakers visit and after field trips to thank the people they met for the experience. Allow for creativity by providing an array of materials and letting the children choose how to create their cards. Ask parents if they have any old wedding announcements, thank-you cards, stationery cards from their workplaces, and envelopes they can donate. This will give you nice cardstock cards with matching envelopes. Simply glue a piece of colored construction paper over the existing cover to give children a fresh slate to create on. Then provide painting supplies, dried flowers, buttons, sequins, and other materials to create cards with. Another recycling idea is to collect old holiday and birthday cards that the children can cut pictures out of to glue onto their new cards. Help them write "Thank You" on the front of each. Keep the cards in a box, and let the children choose an appropriate one for each person you will thank throughout the year. *Activity supports courtesy as children make plans to show gratitude to others, practice writing skills, and participate in a creative activity.*

YOU CAN DEPEND ON ME

Create a poster or letter that children can list three things on under the heading "You Can Depend on Me." Help them think of three things they can help their parents with, such as washing dishes, clearing the table, and putting away their laundry. Write the sentences for them, and then ask the children to draw a picture next to each. Present these to the parents. *Activity supports courtesy as children see themselves as dependable people and supports language skills as they create something to help them talk to parents about.*

CHEER SQUAD

Teach the children this traditional cheer with a twist.

Cheerleader:	I say *please*; you say *thank you*! Please!
Group:	Thank you!
Cheerleader:	Please!
Group:	Thank you!
Cheerleader:	I say *thank you*; you say *you're welcome*! Thank you!
Group:	You're welcome!
Cheerleader:	Thank you!
Group:	You're welcome!

Other combinations: *Achoo* and *bless you*, and *ouch* and *sorry*.

Activity supports courtesy through appropriate language practice.

WHERE'S MY FRIEND MATCH?

Use a set of cards or animal shapes with upper- and lowercase letters, one pair for each letter. Give one uppercase and one lowercase letter to each child, being sure they do not get matching letters. (You can do this with the entire alphabet or break it down and use only a few letters at a time.) Sit the groups of children across from each other. Have the children with the lowercase letters start. One of them holds up a letter card and reads it. For example, "I have an *A*. Where's my friend with the match?" Then the other group checks their cards and the person finding the match holds it up and says, "I'm your friend!" This child hands the match to the first child. Then the child who had the matching card gets a turn; that child reads his or her remaining letter card and repeats the process. The children take turns until all the letters are matched. *Activity supports courtesy through depending on each other for their matches while practicing their letter recognition skills.*

MATH

TOY SORTING

Provide outlines of the shapes of toys on the shelves where they belong. Many programs already do this to encourage children to clean up after themselves, but it can also be a game. When you would like to either change what toys are displayed or rearrange them in the room, create new outlines for the toys and place the outlines in the appropriate places around the room. The toys that belong on the outlines are placed on the floor in the middle of the room. As children arrive, challenge them to pick a toy and find its new home based on its outline. Talk with children about how they can show respect for the items in the room by learning their proper placement and caring for them by putting them away. *Activity supports courtesy through teaching respect and math through matching and classification. Activity also supports creativity through stimulus freedom as it is more typical at arrival time to be taking toys off a shelf rather than putting them away.*

Activity extender: To use this activity to also support language development, use labels with the toys' names rather than outlines. To extend further to new languages, create labels in Spanish or another language you are working on with the children.

FRIEND MATCH GAME

Take photos of the children, taking two pictures (with different poses) of each child. Have the children match together the photos of their friends, naming them as they make the matches. Also, take photos of guest speakers and people the children meet on field trips to add to the match game and help children remember the names of new people they meet. *Activity supports courtesy through respect and remembering the names of those they meet as well as practicing matching skills.*

DIVVY UP THE BLOCKS

Give children hands-on experience with math as well as promote sharing by providing a large bucket of blocks to a small group. Ask them to work together to divvy up the blocks evenly among themselves. When they are finished, ask them how many blocks each child has. Then choose one child to collect all the blocks and divide them up among the children but without keeping any for him- or herself. Again, ask the children to count what they have and discuss the reason behind the difference in numbers. Now make an additional child a collector and have that child and the first collector repeat the task together, further reducing the number of children receiving blocks. Continue the activity until only one child is left and has all of the blocks, and then suggest they play together to create something from their blocks. *Activity supports courtesy through sharing and supports math skills through counting and sorting. Activity also supports curiosity as the children question how many blocks they will get and how changing the number of recipients changes the outcome.*

ACCOMPLISHMENTS CAN ADD UP

Talk with children about respecting others for their accomplishments, how many people work very hard to create or do many things. Provide examples, such as a stack of books by Eric Carle, a set of posters of Picasso paintings, a set of photographs of Frank Lloyd Wright buildings, or class photos of all the children the teacher has taught before. Have the children count them, and then have a discussion about the work that went on to achieve all these accomplishments. *Activity supports courtesy through an understanding of respect for others' accomplishments as well as practicing counting skills.*

JUMPING GEORGE

George Washington always told the truth, but will you? The teacher or parent plays "George" and begins to jump. Children should count how many jumps George takes, and then George says, "I jumped ____ times!" If he is honest, the children all cheer; if he is dishonest, they can boo! Let the children then take turns being George. *Activity supports courtesy through recognition of honesty while practicing counting skills. Activity also supports physical development.*

WHO'S ON FIRST?

Ask the children to line up. For children inexperienced with ordinal numbers, put only four in a line and create as many lines as necessary. Then have them identify their ordinal positions in the line: first, second, third, and so on. Next, pick two children to swap positions. Then have them identify where they are in line again. Repeat this enough times that everyone gets a chance to be first at least once. *Activity supports courtesy through cooperation and practices ordinal-positioning math skills.*

COOKIE SHARE

Whenever you have a lot of items, such as cookies or crackers, and each child will get a few, choose a child to divvy up the items evenly between friends. Try to offer something like this often so each child gets practice in sharing the cookies or crackers fairly. *Activity supports courtesy through sharing and fairness while supporting counting skills.*

WE'RE ALL SPECIAL

Help children understand and respect their similarities and differences. Create a graph and ask the children how many of them _____ and name things they may or may not have in common. For example, how many have brown hair? Blue eyes? How many have sisters? Brothers? How many live in houses? Apartments? How many live in the country? The city? Chart these differences and similarities and talk with the children about the results on the graph. *Activity supports courtesy through an understanding and respect of each others' differences and similarities while supporting math through graphing skills.*

SCIENCE

GET THE BUTTERFLY OUT OF ITS COCOON

This activity is for two children. One child is the caterpillar; the other is the friend. The caterpillar uses a roll of yarn, large scarves, or a roll of toilet paper to wrap around himself and create a cocoon, going around his individual limbs and whole body. When finished, he calls out to his friend—"Please help me! I'm a butterfly now and I need to get out!" The friend comes to help and asks what she can do. The butterfly directs the friend, guiding her to unravel the wrapping, giving encouragement and thanks along the way. The friend follows the directions and asks questions of concern, such as "Does it hurt?" and "Where do I go now?" Model this for the children by first demonstrating it with a child, and then let them pair up to do it on their own.

When finished, the butterfly stretches his "wings," gives a big hug to the friend, says "Thank you!" and flies away. *Activity supports courtesy while children work to help out their friends and practice words of encouragement while actively teaching children about the work a caterpillar goes through to build and come out of a cocoon.*

IS THAT THE RIGHT RECIPE?

How many times have we tried a recipe from a magazine only to have it flop? It's very frustrating because we feel the people at the magazine were being dishonest when they printed it along with a photo of a beautiful, perfect-looking outcome. Children can learn from this same experience. Provide them with recipes that you've changed so that the outcomes will not be successful. Better still, use one you have a photo of (either from a cookbook or one you've taken after you've made the recipe) that looks perfect. Let the children make the recipe as directed. Some nice ones to try are cookies without enough flour, so they go completely flat or a cake or bread with no leavening agent so it does not rise. They make an obvious visual of a mistake. Talk with the children about how they feel when it doesn't come out. Do they feel betrayed?

Then discuss that this is how friends feel when you are not truthful with them. Ask them how they would feel knowing you purposely changed the recipe. Let them know that you did so in order to help them identify and understand how being untruthful can feel, not because you truly wished to betray them. Then remind them that they have discovered that they can learn from mistakes and fix them, and offer them the change that the recipe needs in order to be successful. Let them remake the recipe and celebrate the successful results together! *Activity supports courtesy by building an understanding of honesty and its effects while practicing science skills in recipe making and how different ingredients create different outcomes.*

YOU CAN COUNT ON US

If you don't already have a class pet, the desire to support courtesy in your home or school program should be the motivation you need to make it happen now! Caring for someone other than ourselves is one of the more sure ways to learn kindness and become a dependable person. Some of the easiest pets to care for are goldfish and hermit crabs. Both need only inexpensive food and simple care, such as being in the right light and temperature. Neither habitats need cleaning very often and are easy to clean when they do need it. Both can learn to interact with the children if paid attention to on a regular basis. We had a hermit crab named Jack who would come out of his shell when we called his name and climb up a child's shirt to sit on his or her shoulder. We also had a goldfish who would eat fish food from a child's hand when held at the top of the water. Another would follow a child's finger as it traced the outside of the fish bowl. One would even tap on the side of the bowl whenever music was played! Other pets, such as hamsters, rabbits, and birds, require more extensive habitat cleaning but also offer more interactive fun.

Whatever pet you choose, make a list of things that need to be done in order to care for the pet. Include playing with it and talking to it! Assign these jobs to different children on either a daily or weekly basis. Celebrate any successes, such as when the pet learns something new. Encourage children to learn all they can about their pet by providing books on the subject. *Activity supports courtesy as children learn to be dependable and care for their pet while teaching them about animals, their eating habits, habitat, and capabilities.*

MARY, MARY, QUITE CONTRARY, HOW DOES YOUR GARDEN GROW?

Growing a garden has many benefits, but some of the best are providing an opportunity for children to work cooperatively, learning how the garden depends on them, respecting what is grown, and using what they grow to be kind to others. If you don't have a place to dig a garden, you can build a raised garden with wood or simply fill a small kiddie pool with dirt to make one. If you have no outside space available, you can grow one in window boxes or pots. Vegetables and flowers of all kinds can grow in any of these planters. Be sure to provide seeds for both vegetables and flowers. Each will grow at different speeds, producing an ongoing harvest. Make a list of all the things that need to be done to care for the garden: watering, hoeing, weeding. Assign these jobs to children on a rotating basis. When something is ready to harvest, have the children put it in a basket to deliver to a neighbor, a community helper, a retirement home resident, or other special person. Teach the children that their hard work rewards them not only with produce but with the gratitude of the person they deliver it to, an even bigger reward. *Activity supports courtesy as children learn cooperation, dependability, and kindness while exploring the science of plant growth.*

NATURE WALK

Arrange for either a field trip or a walk to a nature area, such as a park with woods, streams, lakes, prairies, or other natural environments. On this walk, talk with the children about how we can respect nature. For example, we can avoid getting off the trails so we won't crush any of the plants there. We don't pick the flowers, so others can enjoy their beauty. We should take the time to stop and listen and look and appreciate what we hear and see. This type of walk does not give children a close relationship with nature, as discussed early in the book, but it does show children that respect for nature is important. Bring this lesson into an interaction with nature by providing places in your own outdoor environment where children are allowed to dig, pick flowers, and otherwise interact closely with nature. Explain how in public places (such as parks), we must respect nature so it will be there for others to see and experience but that we have places of our own that only we will experience, so we are able to interact with them more closely. *Activity teaches children respect for nature while exploring it with different senses, allowing for observation and then interaction.*

THE BEAR SNORES ON

Read the story *The Bear Snores On*, by Karma Wilson (2002). The story is about a hibernating bear and how little animals come into his cave and share their food while the bear snores on. The bear wakes up, and instead of scaring away the animals, he begins to cry because he's hungry and he's missed the party! But his friends come through and bring out more of their food to share with the bear, and in the end the bear is eating and the friends snore on. Talk with the children about how the friends shared what they had, how they cared about how the bear felt when he woke up. On each page, ask them how the characters feel. Also discuss hibernation— why the bear hibernates, whether the other animals in the story hibernate, and how it feels to wake up from hibernation. After the book and discussion, children can act out the story for even more fun. *Activity supports courtesy as children learn about friendship and explore the feelings of others while providing information regarding hibernation and an interactive learning experience on the subject.*

IS THAT MY FOOD?

Create some matching cards with pictures of animals and the types of food they eat. Talk with the children about these and allow them time to play with them and see if they can find the matches. Then make it more interactive by making masks of different animals and then making pretend food that goes with each. For example, you can make a horse mask and provide some yarn for hay. A cow mask and a small bucket with rice in it for grain. A pig mask and some frozen corn. A lion mask and a plate for a pretend steak. A monkey mask and a banana. Set up a zoo in your space and appoint a zookeeper. Provide a large bag, or better still a wagon, to put all of the animals' food into. Then have the other children put on their masks and pretend to be their animals. As the zookeeper makes his rounds, he or she must find the right food for that animal. *Activity supports courtesy as children learn to respect different food for different animals and learn more about the needs of these animals.*

WORM RESCUE

The next time it rains, check your sidewalk or driveway for worms. Have the children embark on a rescue mission. Give them small buckets to collect the worms in. Then have them take the worms to their garden or a grassy area to let them go. Show the children how to be careful when picking up a worm to show respect for it as a living thing. Use this activity to facilitate an interest in the life of worms, encouraging the children's questions and offering them resources to find the answers.

This same activity can be done on a sunny day when caterpillars come out onto the pavement to get warm. *Activity supports courtesy as children learn respect for living creatures while learning about proper habitat.*

COGNITIVE DEVELOPMENT

HOW CAN WE . . .

Social activities often lend themselves to cooperative problem solving. Take advantage of this and give the children many situations in which they can work together to solve a problem:

How can we rearrange our room?

How can we build a fort?

How can we create a farm?

How can we say thank you to a speaker?

Let the children do some brainstorming and provide them the needed props and materials to put their plan into action. This is a time for very little adult participation! Let the children establish their own structure of leadership and find their own ways to solve the problem together as a group. *Activities promote cooperation between children and cognitive development through problem solving.*

COUNT MY COURTESIES

During a group time, commit acts of kindness and courtesy, such as hugging a child, complimenting someone, saying "please" or "thank you," sharing something, cheering someone on, and so on. At the end of group time, ask the children if they can remember how many acts of kindness or courtesy you committed. *Activity supports courtesy as the adult models courteous behavior and supports cognitive development through memory exercises.*

WHO TOOK THE TEACHER'S APPLE?

In the morning, put an apple on your desk or other prominent place. Talk about its being there in the morning so all of the children are aware of it. At some point in the morning, without the other children noticing, pull aside a child and let him or her in on the plan. Tell the child to take your apple when no one is looking and to put it in the child's cubby or coat pocket. Cover for your accomplice so the child doesn't get caught in the act!

Afterward, pretend to notice that the apple is gone. Ask the children to help you solve the mystery of where the apple went. Let them lead the discussion and come up with ideas. I've had children go from the simple (ask who did it) to the complicated ("We can call Officer Hilliard to come and get fingerprints from the desktop and match them to the children to see who took it"). Let them follow all possible leads. Allow them to work at solving the mystery, providing a new lead only when they reach a dead end, until they find the apple.

Even if they get a confession out of your accomplice, see if they can then figure out where the apple is without being told. Afterward, talk about how taking something that doesn't belong to you is stealing. Let them know that you told the child who took it to do so and that it was okay—the child was not stealing—but discuss how it feels to think someone stole from you and how we should never do this to another person. Congratulate them on solving a mystery and learning more about being good friends! *Activity supports courtesy through an activity that explores honesty and requires cooperation while supporting cognitive development through problem solving.*

WORD HUG

Give the children three words you want them to listen for in a story along with three actions to go with the words, such as hug, shake hands with a neighbor, and clap. Read a story and as you read each word, see how many children remember what the action for that word is. They may get mixed up, and you can help a little, but try to let them remember what the directions were. As you read, more and more children will get it right as they follow their friends. Cheer along with them for their successes! *Activity supports courtesy as children practice kind behaviors while supporting cognitive development through memory activity.*

GRANDMA'S COOKIES FIELD TRIP

Ask the families if they have grandparents who would be open to having the children visit on a field trip. Ask the grandparents to bake their favorite goodie for the children; you bring the milk. Before the field trip, ask the children to come up with questions to ask Grandma and Grandpa. Also ask them to list the polite behaviors they should use while there. Enjoy the field trip, encouraging the grandparents to share stories of their lives and the children to ask questions and to be polite. After the field trip, have the children send a thank-you card that they've made themselves. Have a discussion with the children about what they learned about the people they met, what they liked, and what new things they learned. *Activity supports courtesy as children learn to respect others and work to understand them and know them better. It gives them an opportunity to practice polite and kind behavior during a visit while also developing cognitive skills as they work to create questions and search for answers.*

I'VE LOST MY PLEASES!

In the book *The Children's Book of Virtues* (Bennett, 1995), there is a story titled "Please," by Alicia Aspinwall. Read this to the children. The story is about a little boy whose "please" that lives in his mouth decides he doesn't get used enough, so he jumps into the mouth of the little boy's brother. From then on, the boy cannot say please even when he tries, and his brother always says two pleases in a row. Finally, the please returns and both boys are able to say it once when they need to. Ask the children what they think would happen if they lost their please. Tell them to pretend for one day (and night) to have lost their please. Talk with the parents about it as well. Ask the children to consider other ways to ask politely for something when their please is gone. In the morning, ask everyone how it went at night. Did their parents get upset that they wouldn't say please? Could they find other ways to show politeness? How did it make them feel not to be able to say please? How would they feel if no one else ever said please? *Activity supports courtesy as children explore the reasons for using polite words while supporting cognitive development as they conduct a social experiment and report the results.*

NAUGHTY AND NICE

Create story cards that illustrate choices that are kind and those that are not. You can copy pictures from storybooks that tell this type of story, use clip art from the Internet, or draw your own. Try to create story cards that begin the same way, such as two friends playing together who each have a toy. Make a card that shows one child taking the toy from the other. (Choose an illustration in which it's unclear if one child is giving it or the other child is just taking it.) Then offer two cards for the ending, one where the child whose toy was taken is crying and another where they are both smiling. Put out all the cards and ask the children to use three of them to create a story in sequence. Remember that if you have a creative bunch, they may come up with a sequence that is neither of these two! Rather than look for them to reproduce your sequence, after they have created theirs, ask them to explain the story they made. Any story that makes sense is okay. After they create one story, let them create another. Use the opportunity to talk with them about how they think each child feels in the stories. *Activity supports courtesy through exploration of kindness while supporting cognitive development through sequencing.*

SO HOW DOES IT FEEL?

Create a set of six "feel cups" using large plastic cups with different items in each. Put each cup in a tube sock so the children can reach in the sock and feel what's in the cup but cannot see it. Use items with different textures, such as a pinecone, quarters, cotton balls, beads, yarn, strings, or tinfoil. Have the children sit in a circle. Give each child a cup and choose someone to start. That child is to reach into his or her cup and describe how it feels. The child can either tell the truth or fib. Then the cup is passed to the next child, who feels it and says whether the first child told the truth or fibbed. Then that child describes how it feels. It's possible the first child tells the truth, but the second says it's a fib, and when the second child gives a description it is actually the fib. Continue around the circle, letting each child decide if the previous ones told the truth or fibbed and give a description. Finally, the adult feels in the cup and reveals which children fibbed and which told the truth. *Activity supports courtesy through an activity exploring honesty while supporting cognitive development through sensory exploration.*

HEALTH AND PHYSICAL DEVELOPMENT

BUILD AND LET FRIEND CRASH

During block play, team up two children to play this game. Explain they are to take turns with each role. One child gets to build a tower with the blocks. While building, the second friend waits patiently. When the tower is finished, the builder gives the okay to the other child, who is then allowed to smash down the tower in any fashion he or she likes (kick it, hit it with a hand or ball, and so on). Then they switch positions and repeat. Children learn to build respect for the work of others, and that they should not knock down towers and other creations of others without the builder's permission. *Activity supports courtesy as children learn to respect others' work and supports physical development through motor activity. This activity also supports creativity due to the delayed gratification.*

THE HEALTH BASKET

Talk with the children about the things they need to be healthy: food, clothing, exercise, and so on. Then talk with them about how there are many families who have a hard time getting the things they need in order to stay healthy, that many don't have enough food, warm coats for the winter, or toys such as balls or jump ropes to be active and play with. Get a large box or basket and tell the children you would like to fill a health basket for some families to provide them with things they can use to be healthy. Send a letter home to parents asking them to talk with their children too and to send items such as canned food, gently used coats or other clothing, and toys that encourage active play, such as jump ropes or balls. Ask for just a couple items from each family, and as children bring them, discuss how the items help families stay healthy. Contact your local American Red Cross or other social service agency to donate the box to when it is full. If possible, take a field trip there with the children to donate it together. *Activity supports courtesy as children learn empathy for others while they learn about the things that support healthy living.*

I CAN'T STOP GROWING!

One thing you can always depend on children to do is grow. Talk to them about how they will all continue to grow—it's something they can count on. Illustrate it by measuring the height of each child on a wall, using a sheet of paper over the wall if you don't want to mark the wall. Measure the children every week. Make a growth graph that measures by the eighth-inch. You'll be amazed at how quickly some children grow. I once had a girl who grew a quarter-inch each week for five weeks! Don't focus on the children's actual heights; you don't want it to be a race to be tallest. Rather, focus on how much they have grown from week to week. Do this for at least two months to get a nice visual with your graph of the growing process to discuss with the children. *Activity supports courtesy through a discussion of dependability and supports health and physical development through a better understanding of our bodies and their growth.*

BUCKET BRIGADE

Next time you need to fill the kiddie pool, instead of putting a hose in it, start a bucket brigade! Line up the children between the faucet and the pool, giving each a small bucket. Fill the first child's bucket. That child pours the water into the bucket of the next child in line. They continue to pass the water down the line and dump it into the pool until it is full. *Activity supports courtesy through cooperation while supporting physical development through motor activity. Activity also supports creativity through delayed gratification.*

I CAN JUMP 100 TIMES!

Ask the children to state how many times they think they can jump. Then, one at a time, have them jump while the other children count the jumps. If their numbers were wrong, they should state, "I made a mistake. I can actually jump ____ times." Remind children it is not a matter of lying but that to overstate our capabilities is a type of untruth and we should always strive to be honest about what we can do. At the same time, you want them to know it's okay to be unsure and make a mistake about the number and that it's not a bad thing—the child can simply correct it. *Activity supports courtesy as children explore the aspects of honesty while supporting physical development through large motor activity.*

COAT LINEUP

This is a lot of fun for the children. It teaches them cooperation and kindness while encouraging them to get their coats on for outside play. Ask the children to get their coats and line up but not to put the coats on yet. Tell them about how it is important to their health that they dress appropriately when going outside, so as friends, we want to help each other do this. Then the children should hand their coats to the children behind them, the teacher taking the coat of the last person in line. Now each child holds the coat open so the owner in front can easily slip his or her arms in. Start with the first in line and see how quickly they can help their friends put their coats on. When they get their coats on, encourage them to turn to the children who helped and say "thank you." You can take it a step further and ask them to turn to their friends once more to have the friends zip their coats as well. This will have to start with the first child in line, going one at a time again, so it may take more time. *Activity supports courtesy through kindness and healthy development as children see the importance of dressing appropriately for the outdoors.*

WHO'S FIRST? YOU'RE FIRST!

Next time the children need to line up for something—to wash hands or go outside—have them take a minute to do this fun activity and get a little exercise. After the children line up, have the first one in line turn to the second child and say, "You go first!" and then run to the back of the line. The new first person says the same to the child behind him or her and runs to the back of the line. This continues until everyone has had a chance to be first in line and run to the back, and the child who was originally first is first in line again. Children love to do this as fast as they can, and it's a great way to sneak a little exercise into their day! *Activity supports courtesy through an act of kindness as well as supporting physical development through large motor activity.*

WHY WE WASH OUR HANDS

Obtain a set of Petri dishes donated from a local high school or college or purchased from a science catalog. You will need two dishes for each child.

Hold a discussion about germs and how they stick to our hands. Discuss hand washing and the proper technique. (Singing the ABC's to measure correct time is a standard favorite.) Talk about how we can help our friends to stay healthy by washing our hands and not spreading the germs we pick up. Then explain that you are going to do an experiment to illustrate all the germs we have on our hands. Ask the children to wipe their fingers through the matter in one of their Petri dishes. Put the covers on. Next, have the children wash their hands according to the technique you reviewed. Then have them wipe their cleaned fingers in the other dishes and cover them. Label all covers with the child's name and "before" or "after." Set them on a shelf or table where the children can view them often. Check them daily to see what grows there and to compare the "before" and "after" dishes. Note the different types of bacteria that grow; they will be different shapes and colors. Ask the children to count how many clusters grow in their dishes. Hold a review discussion about the process and the results to see how the children feel about what they learned. *Activity supports courtesy as children consider how their actions can make others sick while supporting an understanding of what makes us sick and how to stay healthy. Activity also supports creativity through delayed gratification.*

THE ARTS

MUSICAL TOYS

This is a game for learning sharing in a fun way. When you bring in some new toys, have the children sit in a circle and hand them the new toys—and some old ones—to play with. Tell them you will be playing some music and that similar to musical chairs, when the music stops, they will need to stop playing with their toys and pass them to the children on their right. The music will play again and when it stops, they pass the toys again, doing this until everyone has had a chance to play with the new toys. The length of time you play the music will depend on the toy. Choose enough time for each child to enjoy the toy before having to pass it on but not so long that the others are unwilling to wait. *Activity supports courtesy as children learn to share while experiencing a musical activity.*

THE GOOD MORNING SONG

To the tune of "Where Is Thumbkin?" ("Frère Jacques"), begin group time by calling the children from play with this song:

Teacher:	Where is (child's name)? Where is (child's name)?
Child:	Here I am! Here I am!
Teacher:	How are you today, (sir or ma'am)?
Child:	Very well. I thank you.
Teacher:	Please come sit. Please come sit.

Repeat the song, calling each child to a place at the group time area. *Activity supports courtesy through modeling of polite conversation while singing.*

FEELINGS COLLAGE

Provide the children with magazines containing pictures that portray many facial expressions. Allow them time to look through the magazines and cut out faces with different expressions. Provide a few examples and a list of emotions and feelings they may see in the photos: scared, surprised, sad, happy, tired, and so on. Help each child find at least four, preferably more. Give them sheets of construction paper and glue so they can make a collage. Either the teacher or the child can then write the name of the feeling on a separate piece of construction paper, cut the word out, and paste it on the collage. *Activity supports courtesy as children work to recognize feelings and emotions of others while creating an art project.*

PAPER SACK PUPPET

Using a brown paper lunch sack, bottom up, have the children create their own puppets. The folded-over bottom becomes the face, with its edge being where the mouth is. Provide lots of materials for them to use, such as construction paper, markers, paints, yarn, fabric, googly (wiggly) eyes, and so on. Ask them to take a moment to figure out what emotion they want to put on their puppets' faces, helping them find ways to reproduce it with the materials they choose. After they have created their puppets, have them put on a puppet show where the puppets get to introduce themselves, talk about how they feel, and then talk with each other. *Activity supports courtesy as children talk about feelings and learn to represent these feelings through tactile art.*

FEELINGS PLAY

Give the children an assortment of costumes to choose from for a play. They can become any people or animals they like, and they need to decide how their characters are going to feel during the play: surprised, sad, tired, mad, and so on—any emotion except happy. Ask one child to be the traveler, who is walking down a road to a village. The traveler will meet many villagers (and possibly animals) along the way. It is the traveler's job to get to know them and help them be happy again. Let the children take it from there by sending out one at a time to meet the traveler along the way. Allow them to create their own dialog based on the feelings they chose and the traveler to problem solve to help the other character be happy again. Once happy, the villager or animal can join the traveler on the journey. *Activity supports courtesy as children practice understanding the feelings of others and being kind in helping them while participating in the arts through acting.*

I HAVE A FRIEND SONG

This is a fun song to do at circle time, starting with one child and working clockwise around the circle until everyone has had a chance. Or it can be used to call children to circle time. The teacher begins by calling one child. Then that child sings the song to call over another child and so on until all of the children have joined the circle. It's sung to the tune of "Paw, Paw, Patch."

> I have a friend and her (or his) name is (child's name).
>
> I have a friend and her (or his) name is (child's name).
>
> I have a friend and her (or his) name is (child's name).
>
> She (or he) likes me and I like her (or him)!

Activity supports courtesy as children identify friends while supporting the arts through music.

A RAINBOW OF FEELINGS

Provide each child with a large sheet of butcher paper to paint on. It can be put on an easel or table or on the floor. Give them large paintbrushes at least two inches wide and cups of paint in six different colors, which each child will use only once. Ask the children to choose a color that represents how they feel when they are happy. Then have them dip their brushes in that color and paint one wide and long stripe on the far left of their paper. Next they should pick a color that represents them feeling mad. Again, have them paint one long stripe, this one next to the first one. Next a color that represents tired. Then surprised. Then sad. Finally, worried. They should have used all of their colors and have a sheet of paper with six long stripes on it. Ask them to step back and take a look around the room to see the paintings their friends have made. Did everyone create the same sequence of colors? Or are the rainbows different? Ask some of them to discuss why they chose the colors that they did. *Activity supports courtesy through an exploration of feelings while supporting the arts through artistic expression of these feelings using color.*

GROUP PAINTING

Cover the entire table the children are working at with a strip of butcher paper. If you have a large group with several tables, cover each table. Let the children know they are going to produce a mural, a very large painting that they will be making together. They can paint anything they like on the mural, but they are to be respectful of each other's work and not paint over something someone else has done. They should also be mindful of the empty areas and ask each other if someone else plans to paint in that space. Working together, they should try to paint something on every inch of the paper so it is completely covered. They are more than welcome to decide on one picture they can all

Web Sites for Lesson Plans on Character Development

www.teacherplanet.com

www.goodcharacter.com

www.livingvalues.net

paint together or decide to work in their own areas. Allow them time to discuss among themselves what they would like to do and make a collective decision before starting. When they are finished, hang the murals on the wall or in a hallway for the children to show their parents. *Activity supports courtesy through cooperation and respect for others' work while participating in an artistic activity.*

References

Beck, J. (1999). *How to raise a brighter child.* New York: Pocket Books.

Bennett, W. J. (Ed.). (1995). *The children's book of virtues.* New York: Simon & Schuster.

Benson, P. L., Galbraith, J., & Espeland, P. (1998). *What kids need to succeed.* Minneapolis, MN: Free Spirit.

Berman, J. (2007). *The A to Z guide to raising happy, confident kids.* Novato, CA: New World Library.

Bilhartz, T. (1999). *Study shows music training improves intelligence.* Retrieved from Sam Houston State University Web site: www.shsu.edu/~pin_www/T@S/1999/EarlyMus.html.

Carle, E. (1969). *The very hungry caterpillar.* New York: Philomel Books.

Carlson, G. (2008). *Child of wonder: Nurturing creative and curious children.* Eugene, OR: Common Ground Press.

Cuyler, M. (2004). *Please say please! Penguin's guide to manners.* New York: Scholastic.

Dacey, J., & Packer, A. (1992). *The nurturing parent: How to raise creative, loving, responsible children.* New York: Simon & Schuster.

Dodge, D. T., Colker, L. J., & Heroman, C. (2002). *The Creative Curriculum for preschool* (4th ed.). Washington, DC: Teaching Strategies.

Drew, W., Christie, J., Johnson, J. E., Meckley, A. M., & Nell, M. (2008). Constructive play: A value-added strategy for meeting early learning standards. *Young Children, 63*(4), 38–44.

Dr. Seuss. (1990). *Oh, the places you'll go!* New York: Random House.

Eberly, S. (2001). *365 manners kids should know.* New York: Three Rivers Press.

Fields, H. B. (2009). *Don't cheat the children: Connecting generations through grand friendships.* Downers Grove, IL: Wonderstone Press.

Gardner, H. (1993). *Creating minds.* New York: Basic Books.

Ginsburg, M. (1975). *How the sun was brought back to the sky.* New York: Macmillan.

Helm, J. H. (2008). Don't give up on engaged learning. *Young Children, 63*(4), 14–20.

Kara-Soteriou, J., & Rose, H. (2008). A bat, a snake, a cockroach, and a fuzzhead: Using children's literature to teach about positive character traits. *Young Children, 63*(4), 30–35.

Keeler, R. (2008). *Natural playscapes: Creating outdoor play environments for the soul*. Redmond, WA: Exchange Everyday.

Leffert, N., Benson, P. L., & Roehlkepartain, J. L. (1997). *Starting out right*. Minneapolis, MN: Search Institute.

Lobel, A. (1963). *A holiday for Mister Muster*. New York: Harper & Row.

Louv, R. (2005). *Last child in the woods*. Chapel Hill, NC: Algonquin Books.

Markova, D. (1991). *The art of the possible*. San Francisco: Conari Press.

McElmeel, S. L. (2002). *Character education*. Greenwood Village, CO: Teacher Ideas Press.

Pink, D. (2006). *A whole new mind*. New York: Berkley.

Post, P. (2002). *Emily Post's the gift of good manners: A parent's guide to raising respectful, kind, considerate children*. New York: HarperResource.

Relf, A. (2005). *Fox makes friends*. New York: Scholastic.

Slater, G. (2008, Fall). He's committed to leaving no child indoors. *Wisconsin Early Childhood Association Newsletter*, p. 13.

Snyder, G. (2006). *More help! For teachers of young children*. Thousand Oaks, CA: Corwin.

Solomon, P. G. (2003). *The curriculum bridge: From standards to actual classroom practice*. Thousand Oaks, CA: Corwin.

Wallace, C. (1996). *The modern guide to teaching children good manners*. New York: St. Martin's.

Wilson, K. (2002). *The bear snores on*. New York: Scholastic.

Subject Index

Index of Activities by State Standards

173

CORWIN
A SAGE Company

The Corwin logo—a raven striding across an open book—represents the union of courage and learning. Corwin is committed to improving education for all learners by publishing books and other professional development resources for those serving the field of PreK–12 education. By providing practical, hands-on materials, Corwin continues to carry out the promise of its motto: **"Helping Educators Do Their Work Better."**